READY-TO-USE
MUSIC ACTIVITIES
KIT

Ready-to-Use
Music Activities
Kit

Audrey J. Adair

Illustrated by Leah Solsrud

Parker Publishing Company, Inc.

West Nyack, New York

© 1984 by

Parker Publishing Company, Inc.

West Nyack, New York

Library of Congress Cataloging in Publication Data

Adair, Audrey J.
    Ready-to-use music activities kit.

    1. School music—Instruction and study.
2. Music—Theory, Elementary.   I. Solsrud, Leah.
II. Title.
MT10.A15   1984   372.8'7044   83-17480
ISBN 0-13-762295-3

Printed in the United States of America

ABOUT THE AUTHOR

Audrey Adair has taught music at all levels in the Houston, Texas and Dade County, Florida public schools. She has served as a music consultant, music specialist, general music instructor, choir director, and classroom teacher. In addition, she has written a series of musical programs for assemblies and holiday events, organized music programs for the community, established Glee Club organizations, and did specialization work with the hearing impaired, the educable, trainable, and severely mentally retarded, as well as orthopedically handicapped children.

Mrs. Adair received her B.A. Degree in Music Education from St. Olaf College in Minnesota and completed post baccalaureate work at the University of Houston and Florida Atlantic University in Ft. Lauderdale.

ABOUT THIS KIT

The purpose of the READY-TO-USE MUSIC ACTIVITIES KIT is to give music specialists and classroom music teachers a variety of highly motivating, ready-to-use activities to spark children's involvement in music while reinforcing basic music skills and concepts.

Between its covers you will find 214 different music activities within the major subject areas of the elementary music curriculum, all conveniently organized into 14 topical sections. Each activity represents a written exercise to be performed by the individual student, emphasizing one specific area of music education or skill. Moreover, each is confined to a single page, is designed to be completed within a typical class period, and can be photocopied as many times as needed for classroom use.

The written exercises are presented in a diversity of formats, including anagrams, crossword puzzles, word finders, illustrations, word and symbol matching, and others. They were developed with the entire class in mind, but are equally suitable for use with individual students or small groups. Each activity has been successfully tested with students of varying degrees of musical ability and background. Together, the varied activities contained in the KIT will help you recognize individual differences and provide a well-balanced music curriculum.

You will find these activities require little or no advance preparation on your part. However, for most effective use, it is recommended that you fully explore the activity pages before using them. Each activity is meant to be an integral part of your subject matter, for example, listening, playing instruments, singing, or composing. While introducing an activity, it is suggested that you read the information provided for the activity in the "Teacher's Guide and Answer Key" at the end of the particular section. Included under each activity title are complete answer keys and, in many cases, background information and procedures for using the activity.

The activities within each of the 14 sections of the KIT are generally sequenced by increasing degrees of difficulty. Beginning activities are easy enough to assure success. More challenging activities follow and are designed to extend a previously introduced concept. The language used in the activities is simple, and any unfamiliar terms are explained in a straightforward manner. Moreover, most activities are enhanced by drawings that help to relay the particular concept and also serve to motivate students.

To simplify recordkeeping and evaluation, a progress chart is provided at the end of the introduction ("To the Teacher") and complete answer keys are given in the "Teacher's Guide and Answer Key" at the end of each section. The Key is constructed in a format that permits grading by either the student or teacher. Certain activities are self-checking.

For all teachers of elementary school music, the READY-TO-USE MUSIC ACTIVITIES KIT offers a well-organized, easy-to-use collection of music activities to accompany daily lesson plans. These free the teacher to work with individual children while providing effective and fun-filled music experiences for the entire class. I hope that you and your students enjoy these activities and that they allow you to spend more time where it is most needed. Good teaching!

Audrey J. Adair

TO THE TEACHER

Whether you are a music specialist or a classroom teacher in charge of your own music program, the READY-TO-USE MUSIC ACTIVITIES KIT will be an invaluable addition to your music curriculum. It contains over 200 stimulating music activities in the form of student worksheets, each ready for duplication and classroom use. These activities will help you add new "spark" to your music classes and provide an excellent way to involve all of your students in music while reinforcing basic skills and concepts.

A Year-Round Music Activities Program

The activities in the KIT were developed to meet the needs of a full-year elementary music curriculum. The content includes a comprehensive study of basic skills in music that emphasizes DOING, including sections on music theory, singing, composing, listening, ear training, and instruments of the band and orchestra. A quick glance at the Table of Contents will show you the wide range of activities which integrate these many facets of music into a total learning experience.

The activity worksheets depart from the conventional question-and-answer method and add a new dimension to learning by involving the child totally in the lesson. Headed by provocative titles, they are presented in a variety of different formats, including anagrams, crossword puzzles, word finders, and matching exercises.

For quick access, the activities are organized into 14 distinct sections categorized according to specific subject matter. Within each section the worksheets are arranged in sequential order to allow for varying levels of ability. Although each activity can stand alone, it is treated not as a separate or detached part, but is seen in its relationship to the entire structure of music. The focus is on one main concept per activity and the presentation is easy to follow.

Appropriate for All Age and Ability Levels

The student worksheets have been tested in the classroom and proven suitable for students of different ability and age levels. They include many activities for the beginner as well as for the student who already possesses some musical knowledge. Some of the activities are simple and repetitious enough for the early grades, while others will interest and challenge students in the middle school. All are short, confined to one page for easy duplication, and designed to be finished in one class period.

The language used throughout the KIT is easy to understand and helps take the mystery out of music terminology. The vocabulary has been carefully checked so that even the lower-level elementary student should have no difficulty in reading and/or understanding most of the activities. Over 175 music terms are clearly defined on the worksheets.

Each activity provides clear, step-by-step student directions. Many worked-out sample problems show the student how to proceed. Imaginative drawings and informative charts and graphs add visual impact and help to explain music terms and concepts. The activities help to create an environment in which all children, on all skill levels, can find music more rewarding and enjoyable.

Adaptable to a Variety of Instructional Needs

You will find that the activities are easily adapted to many instructional purposes, including pre-skill testing, reteaching, extra practice, enrichment lessons, and imaginative drills. Different worksheets may be assigned as homework or used for review, motivational, or remedial purposes. Evaluation activities are spaced throughout the KIT to give you feedback on students' understanding of basic skills and concepts.

While the activities were developed for use with an entire class, they are also appropriate for a learning center situation and for small group or individual instruction. Moreover, they can be used effectively with all children, from the special learner to the child who is gifted in music.

The KIT covers music from various places, different periods, and many ethnic groups. Many of the songs are arranged in simple melody line form with lyrics and chords suitable for guitar, autoharp, and piano. A variety of seasonal material is included, too.

Recordkeeping and Evaluation Aids

To help you keep an accurate record of the activities completed, a "Progress Chart" is provided on pages xiii through xxi. The chart lists all activities and corresponding skills. You may write in individual names or classes and check off each activity and skill when it is completed. The chart gives you an overall view of your basic teaching plan and will keep you in touch with the progress your students are making toward mastery of a particular music skill or concept.

Regarding evaluation, certain activities are designed for self-checking. These are marked with an "s/c" on the Progress Chart. As for checking the other worksheets, you may want to have each student check his or her own work and make the necessary corrections at that time. The answer keys may be copied and placed at a central location for this purpose. Completed worksheets may be kept in individual folders so they can be studied from time to time.

Teacher's Guide and Answer Keys

The "Teacher's Guide and Answer Key" at the end of each section of the KIT provides complete answers for each activity in that section as well as background information and teaching suggestions for presenting certain activities to your students. Activities designated with an asterisk include explicit directions for getting the most out of them. These activities may be correlated with different worksheets throughout the KIT for reteaching specific concepts or skills. You may find, for example, that repetition of important concepts, skills, and ideas will help you measure your students' growth.

Special Instructional Uses

The activities in the KIT will be useful to instrumental, piano, and vocal teachers as well as to the elementary music specialist and the classroom music teacher.

For the instrumental teacher, the music theory portion of the KIT provides help in teaching note-reading. Often a student starts playing an instrument with little or no previous instruction in note-reading. The teacher must thus start from "scratch," teaching the rudiments. The basic music concepts emphasized in the KIT constitute a complete note-reading program.

The activities focusing on the orchestra and its families of instruments are another useful source for the instrumental teacher. They include many fine illustrations of orchestral instruments and folk instruments which are virtually guaranteed to promote enthusiasm among your students. The section on instruments offers a stimulating way to explore the sights and sounds of both the band and the symphony orchestra.

The piano teacher will find many activities of value, too. Illustrations of the piano keyboard are used to introduce all aspects of music theory, from lines and spaces, rhythms, intervals, chords, and time signatures, to forming major and minor scales. These activities take the dullness and complexity out of learning to note-read and make effective written assignments for home study. The easy-to-read directions in each activity tell the student exactly how to complete the lesson.

The vocal teacher will find the KIT an enduring aid, not only for the variety of songs covered in the activities, but also for the wealth of material included for the individual with no vocal background or musical training. The teacher need simply select the appropriate activities and duplicate them as many times as required for class or individual use.

PROGRESS CHART

Use this chart to keep a record of activities completed for each class. List your classes in the given spaces at the right. For eight classes you will need two copies. As each activity is completed for a class mark an X in the appropriate column.

(NOTE: An "S/C" after an activity title indicates "self-checking.")

I. LEARN A FEW BASICS

No.	Activity Title	Skill Involved	Classes			
1.	MATCH 'EM	Analyzing the staff				
2.	FIND A "CRUTCH"	Analyzing the staff				
3.	DRAW THE NOTES	Drawing line and space notes				
4.	NAME THE NOTES	Naming the notes				
5.	A DRAWING CONTEST	Drawing clef signs				
6.	ADDING LINES	Drawing leger lines				
7.	NOTE REVIEW	Reviewing letter names of notes				
8.	SUM IT UP (S/C)	Testing basics				

II. LET'S READ NOTES

No.	Activity Title	Skill Involved				
1.	THE NOTE SPELLDOWN (S/C)	Naming notes on the staff				
2.	PRETENDING (S/C)	Naming notes on the staff				
3.	CATCH A FISH (S/C)	Naming notes—crossword puzzle				
4.	COMPLETE THE STORY (S/C)	Naming notes—musical story				
5.	MUSICAL SPELLING (S/C)	Making words from note names				
6.	CAN YOU NAME THEM?	Naming instruments from note names				
7.	READ A SECRET NOTE	Identifying letter names of notes				
8.	O.K., MESSAGE RECEIVED	Making words from note names				
9.	MORE MESSAGES TO DECODE	Recognizing notes by name				
10.	A CAGEY PROBLEM (S/C)	Naming notes—musical story				
11.	WHAT HAPPENS NEXT?	Naming notes—musical story				
12.	CROSSWORD PUZZLE	Writing words from notes				
13.	MORE NOTES TO NAME (S/C)	Writing letter names for notes				
14.	SPELL THE WORDS	Recognizing notes by name				
15.	DRAWING NOTES	Drawing notes				
16.	LEARNING ABOUT THE KEYBOARD	Recognizing the order of the keys				
17.	WRITE THE NAMES	Learning the musical alphabet on the keyboard				

IV. FIGURING DURATION

No.	Activity Title	Skill Involved				
			Classes			
5.	BALANCE THE SCALES	Drawing equal notes or rests				
6.	KNOW YOUR NOTES	Reviewing note values				
7.	THE REST IS UP TO YOU	Drawing the missing rests on the staff				
8.	PLAYING MUSICAL DOMINOS	Decoding time values				
9.	ADD A DOT	Recognizing dotted notes and their time values				
10.	NOTE SEARCH	Finding two notes which equal a dotted note				
11.	MUSICAL MATH	Adding note values				

V. LOOKING AT METER SIGNATURES

No.	Activity Title	Skill Involved				
1.	ACCENT THE BEAT	Identifying accented beats				
2.	WRITE THE METER SIGNATURES (S/C)	Writing meter signatures				
3.	DOES IT MEASURE UP?	Drawing bar lines to match Meter Signatures				
4.	DRAW THE MATCHING NOTES	Analyzing $\frac{4}{4}$ time.				
5.	WHAT'S THE TIME? (S/C)	Writing $\frac{4}{4}$, $\frac{3}{4}$ and $\frac{2}{4}$ Meter Signatures				
6.	REWRITE THE SONG	Rewriting a song using different meter				
7.	DIP, DIP AND SWING	Completing a song by adding bar lines and a double bar				
8.	A METER QUIZ	Analyzing the bottom number of the meter				
9.	BE A BETTER METER READER	Drawing the missing notes				
10.	THE TREASURE HUNT	Rewriting measures in the correct order				
11.	UPBEAT VS. DOWNBEAT	Making up final measures for songs with a pickup				
12.	CHOOSE THE ANSWER (S/C)	Testing Meter Signature knowledge				
13.	FIND THE MEASURES	Reviewing facts				
14.	CROSS IT OUT	Interpreting Compound Meter				
15.	SUPPLY THE MISSING NOTES	Reviewing Time Signatures and completing measures				
16.	WHAT'S THE BOTTOM NUMBER?	Writing the denominator for different Meter Signatures				
17.	DO THEY MEASURE UP?	Completing measures with different meters				

VI. EXAMINING SCALES AND KEY SIGNATURES

No.	Activity Title	Skill Involved				Classes
16.	OBEY THE ORDER (S/C)	Drawing and memorizing the order of sharps				
17.	LEARN THE LINE-UP	Drawing and memorizing the order of flats				
18.	BUILD MAJOR SCALES IN SHARPS	Writing scales using up to four sharps				
19.	BUILD MAJOR SCALES IN FLATS	Writing scales using up to four flats				
20.	THINK THE NOTE ABOVE (S/C)	Writing ♯ key signatures and naming tonic key				
21.	FIND THE KEY IN FLATS (S/C)	Naming ♭ key signatures and drawing the keynote				
22.	DRAW THE SHARPS	Drawing correct number of sharps				
23.	DRAW THE FLATS	Drawing correct number of flats				
24.	"B" SHARP	Writing scales using sharps and marking half steps				
25.	DOWN WITH FLATS	Writing scales using flats and marking half steps				
26.	CROSSWORD PUZZLE (S/C)	Reviewing facts—crossword puzzle				
27.	COMPLETE THE SENTENCES (S/C)	Recalling facts				
28.	BUILD THE SCALE STEPPER (S/C)	Recalling facts—puzzle				
29.	QUIZ ON SCALES	Writing key signatures and scales				
30.	MEET THE MINORS	Examining natural minor and harmonic scales				
31.	DOUBLE OR NOTHING	Remembering facts				

VII. IDENTIFYING INTERVALS

No.	Activity Title	Skill Involved				
1.	WRITE THE LETTER (S/C)	Recognizing steps, skips and repeats				
2.	DRAW THE NOTE	Drawing 2nds, 3rds and repeated notes				
3.	THINK UP, DOWN, OR SAME	Drawing notes to show: step, skip or repeat				
4.	WHICH: MELODIC OR HARMONIC?	Distinguishing between melodic and harmonic				
5.	USE THE NUMBERS	Drawing top notes for harmonic intervals				
6.	STEP, SKIP, OR REPEAT (S/C)	Recognizing intervals				
7.	UNLOCK THE "OCT" (S/C)	Understanding the word octave				
8.	OVERLOOKING OCTAVES	Identifying and completing octaves				

IX. BE A COMPOSER

No. Activity Title	Skill Involved	Classes			
4. FIND THE ERRORS (S/C)	Correcting a tune				
5. REWRITE THE TUNE	Rewriting a rhythm pattern with different notes				
6. DO IT DIFFERENTLY	Adding a measure with different rhythm				
7. QUESTION +ANSWER = PERIOD	Identifying phrases				
8. CAN I COMPOSE?	Constructing a melody				

X. LEARNING TO LISTEN

No. Activity Title	Skill Involved				
1. YOUR OPINION, PLEASE (S/C)	Identifying listening skills				
2. HOW DO YOU LISTEN? (S/C)	Examining listening skills				
3. BROADEN YOUR APPRECIATION	Answering thought questions on music appreciation				
4. WHAT'S YOUR ATTITUDE? (S/C)	Evaluating types of listening				

XI. TRAINING YOUR EAR

No. Activity Title	Skill Involved				
1. BASS OR TREBLE? (S/C)	Recognizing high and low sounds				
2. WHAT DO YOU HEAR (S/C)	Hearing sound direction				
3. LISTEN AND CHECK (S/C)	Hearing and recognizing measures				
4. "RIGHT THEM"	Rewriting notes in right order				
5. LISTEN TO THE BEAT (S/C)	Hearing and locating the incorrect measure				
6. HOW'S YOUR HEARING?	Hearing which notes are played				
7. CHOOSE THE PATTERN (S/C)	Selecting the correct musical pattern				
8. DECIDE THE METER (S/C)	Conducting and writing the meter				
9. IDENTIFY THE INTERVALS	Distinguishing between melodic and harmonic intervals				
10. CHECK THE SCALES (S/C)	Identifying altered notes in Major scales				
11. PICK THE TUNE (S/C)	Recognizing beginning melody patterns				
12. STEP, SKIP, OR REPEAT?	Hearing and notating steps, skips, and repeats				
13. JUDGE THE MUSIC	Identifying pitch direction on the keyboard				
14. DRAW THE INSTRUMENT	Drawing the instrument you hear being played				

CONTENTS

Section I
LEARN A FEW BASICS

1. MATCH 'EM

The word STAFF has many meanings, and in music it has a special meaning. The set of lines and spaces on which music is written is called a STAFF. Each staff has five lines and four spaces. Learn more about the staff by reading the information below.

For each pair of boxes, fill in the second box so it matches the first one. Then complete the sentences at the bottom of the page by writing in the missing words.

5 LINES + 4 SPACES = STAFF

The lines of the staff are horizontal and the same distance apart.

LINES

The lines are always counted from the bottom of the staff to the top.

SPACES

The spaces are always counted from the bottom of the staff to the top.

1. A staff is made up of _____ _____ and _____ _____.

2. The lines are always counted from the _____ of the staff to the _____.

3. The spaces are always counted from the _____ of the staff to the _____.

4. The third space is _____ (higher/lower) than the third line.

5. The second line is _____ (higher/lower) than the second space.

2. FIND A "CRUTCH"   (I–2)

Music language uses the first seven letters of the alphabet: A B C D E F G. After G, the letter names start again with A: A B C D E F G <u>A</u> <u>B</u> <u>C,</u> and so on.

The lines and spaces of the staff have letter names. Learn more about the letter names by reading and completing the work below. You will find a "crutch" to help you remember the letter names of the lines and spaces.

For each pair of boxes, fill in the second box so it matches the first one.

The letter names of the spaces are F A C E.

The letter names of the lines are E G B D F.

To help you remember the names of the spaces, think of what F A C E spells—of course, face. To remember the names of the lines E G B D F, use them as the beginning letters of words in a sentence. The following two sentences are examples. Underline the beginning letter of each word.

a. Every good boy deserves fudge.   b. Empty garbage before Dad flips.

Write two sentences of your own to help you remember the names of the lines. Check your sentences by underlining the first letter of each word. Do they spell E G B D F?

1.

2.

3. The letter names of the spaces spell the word_____.

4. The letter names of the lines are _____ _____ _____ _____ _____.

3. DRAW THE NOTES   (I–3)

Music is written with a STAFF and NOTES. The notes stand for musical sounds or tones.

There are two steps to making a note. The top part is drawn first and then the bottom part. Trace over the lines to make the note below.

Top part   +   bottom part   =   note

Draw two lines of notes using the two steps in the example above:

There are both LINE NOTES and SPACE NOTES.

When a line goes through a note, it is called a LINE NOTE.

A note without a line through it is called a SPACE NOTE.

Draw a Line Note.

Draw a Space Note.

These are examples of Line Notes on the staff.

These are examples of Space Notes on the staff.

Draw three Line Notes on the staff.

Draw three Space Notes on the staff.

On the staff below, mark all Line Notes with an "X" and circle all Space Notes.

4. NAME THE NOTES   (I–4)

1. a. Draw a Line Note.   b. Draw a Space Note.

2. There are both Line Notes and Space Notes on the staff below. On the spaces under the staff, write an "L" for each Line Note, and an "S" for each Space Note.

3. You have learned that the lines and spaces of the staff have letter names. Notes that are found on the lines and spaces take on their letter names. For example, a note on the "F" space is called the "F" NOTE, a note on the "G" line is called the "G" NOTE, and so on.

   a. Find the Line Notes on the staff. Write their letter names below in the order they appear. (The answer spells a word.)

   b. Find the Space Notes on the staff. Write their letter names below in the order they appear. (The answer spells a word.)

4. On the staff below, draw the proper notes above the letter names.

   $(NOTE = \wedge + \cup = O)$

   G   E   F   A   D   B   C   A   G   B

Name _____   Score _____

Date _____   Class _____

5. A DRAWING CONTEST

Signs called CLEFS are used at the beginning of every line of music. They tell us whether a piece of music is for high or low voices or instruments.

This is the TREBLE or G CLEF. Music in this clef is for the higher (children's or women's) voices and instruments, the guitar, and the right hand of the piano and other keyboard instruments.

The Treble or G Clef gives us the position for the note "G" on the second line. Notice how the curved line of the clef draws a ring around the second line.

A staff with this clef sign is called the TREBLE STAFF.

An important part of musical training is to be able to write music that is plain and clear, and easy to read. Six steps in drawing the Treble Clef are shown below. Trace the lines of the Treble Clef for each step.

Following the above steps, draw ten Treble Clef signs as neatly as you can on the staff below.

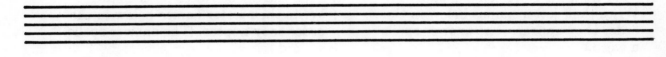

This is the BASS or F CLEF. Music in this clef is for the lower voices and instruments, and the left hand of the piano and other keyboard instruments. This clef also gives us the position for the "F" note. The "head" of the clef rests on the fourth line, which is F. The other notes run in order up and down the staff, with G in the space above F, and so on.

A staff with this clef sign is called the BASS STAFF.

In the space below, draw a staff with the Bass Clef sign.

6. ADDING LINES   (I–6)

You have learned about Line Notes and Space Notes. Notes may also be written above and below the staff, and on short lines called LEGER LINES. These lines extend the staff. They are necessary because most instruments and voices cover more notes than can be shown on the five lines and four spaces of the staff.

Leger lines have the same distance between them as the lines of the staff. They are just long enough to extend slightly to each side of the note.

Study the placement of the Leger Lines and notes on the staffs below. Complete the second staff of each pair to match the first one.

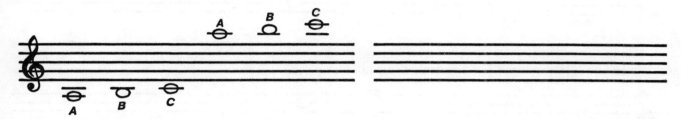

When you sing or play notes that are above "high F," these notes are written in the spaces above the staff and on Leger Lines. These notes are read in exactly the same way as the notes you have already seen. If F is on the line, G will be in the space above, A is on the next line, and so on.

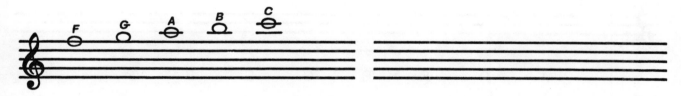

When you sing or play notes that are below the Treble Staff, these notes are written in the spaces below the staff and on Leger Lines. The note called "Middle C" is on the first Leger Line below the staff.

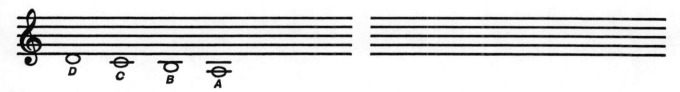

Draw a staff with a Treble Clef sign. Put in all the notes from "Middle C" to "C" on the second Leger Line above the staff. Name the notes.

Name _____   Score _____

Date _____   Class _____

7. NOTE REVIEW   (I–7)

1. Name the Line Notes.   2. Name the Space Notes.

3. Draw the Treble Clef on the staff below and write the letter names of the notes.

4. Write the letter names for the following notes.

5. Draw the proper note above each letter name on the staff below.

       A   D   F   E   C   G   B   F

6. On the above staff, mark the Line Notes with an "X" and circle all the Space Notes.

8. SUM IT UP   (I–8)

The following story "sums up" some of the things you have learned about music. Write in the missing words or letters.

Music is written on a _____ (1) with _____ (2). The staff is a set of five _____ (3) and four _____ (4). Lines and spaces both have letter _____ (5). The letter names of the spaces are _____ (6). To remember the names of the spaces, think of the word _____ (7). The letter names of the lines are ____ ____ ____ ____ ____ (8). Sometimes it is helpful to remember a "crutch" for the names of the lines. You can use these letters as the beginning letters of words in a _____ (9). One sentence that uses this "crutch" is: "Empty garbage before Dad _____ (10)." The beginning letters for each word in this sentence name the lines and they are: ____ ____ ____ ____ ____ (11).

There are Line Notes and _____ (12) Notes. When a line goes through a note, it is called a _____ (13) Note. When a note doesn't have a line going through it, it is called a _____ (14) Note.

Clef signs are used at the beginning of every musical _____ (15). Another name for the Treble Clef is the _____ (16) Clef. The Bass Clef is used for the lower _____ (17) in piano music.

The staff is extended with the use of Leger _____ (18). The first added line below the staff is named _____ (19). The first added line above the staff is named _____ (20).

The musical alphabet has the following letter names: _____ (21). Notes have the same letter names as the lines and _____ (22). If the note "G" is on a line, _____ (23) is in the space above, _____ (24) is on the next line, and so on.

It is helpful to know basic facts about music if you are going to be good at reading _____ (25).

TEACHER'S GUIDE
AND ANSWER KEY

1. *Match 'Em*

    1. 5 lines, 4 spaces   2. bottom, top   3. bottom, top   4. higher   5. lower

2. *Find a "Crutch"*

Introduce the term *Musical Alphabet*, which refers to the first seven letters of the alphabet. Discuss what *crutch* means (an aid).

    3. F A C E   4. E G B D F

3. *Draw the Notes*

4. *Name the Notes*

    2. L, S, L, S, L, L, S, S, S, S   3. a. BEGGED   b. FACE
    4. (Some notes will appear twice on the staff.)

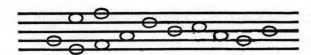

5. *A Drawing Contest*

Children will determine what the drawing contest is for (to determine who can draw the neatest clef signs). Explain that when the two staffs are used, the treble staff appears above the bass staff.

6. *Adding Lines*

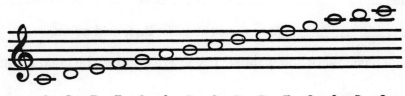

C D E F G A B C D E F G A B C

10

7. Note Review

1. E G B D F 2. F A C E 3. C D E F G A B C 4. B F C F D A G D
5.–6.

A D F E C G B F

8. Sum It Up

Explain that when the term "staff" is used alone, it refers to the treble staff.

1. staff	7. Face	13. Line	19. "C"
2. notes	8. E G B D F	14. Space	20. "A"
3. lines	9. sentence	15. staff	21. A B C D E F G
4. spaces	10. flips	16. "G"	22. spaces
5. names	11. E G B D F	17. notes	23. A
6. F A C E	12. space	18. Lines	24. B
			25. notes

Section II
LET'S READ NOTES

TEACHER'S GUIDE AND ANSWER KEY

1. THE NOTE SPELLDOWN

(II-1)

Write the letter names for the following notes.*

* Check your answers by reading the note names from the top to the bottom. Each group of letters spells a word.

Write the words here:

1. _____   2. _____   3. _____

4. _____   5. _____   6. _____

Name _____   Score _____

Date _____   Class _____

2. PRETENDING   (II–2)

Write the letter name for each of the following notes. Each group of notes spells the name of a boy or girl.

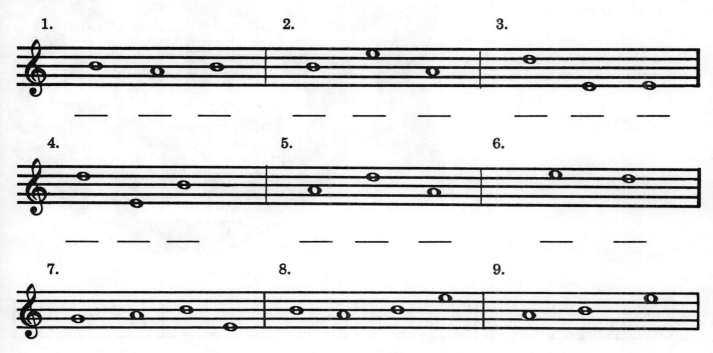

1.   ___ ___ ___   2.   ___ ___ ___   3.   ___ ___ ___

4.   ___ ___ ___   5.   ___ ___ ___   6.   ___ ___ ___

7.   ___ ___ ___ ___   8.   ___ ___ ___ ___   9.   ___ ___ ___

Pretend you have a friend among the children below. Choose a name from the above group and write it under his or her picture.

Name _____   Score _____

Date _____   Class _____

3. CATCH A FISH

You've caught yourself a fish if you can spell the words. How's your bait? Good luck!

Read the notes below and then write the words on the puzzle.

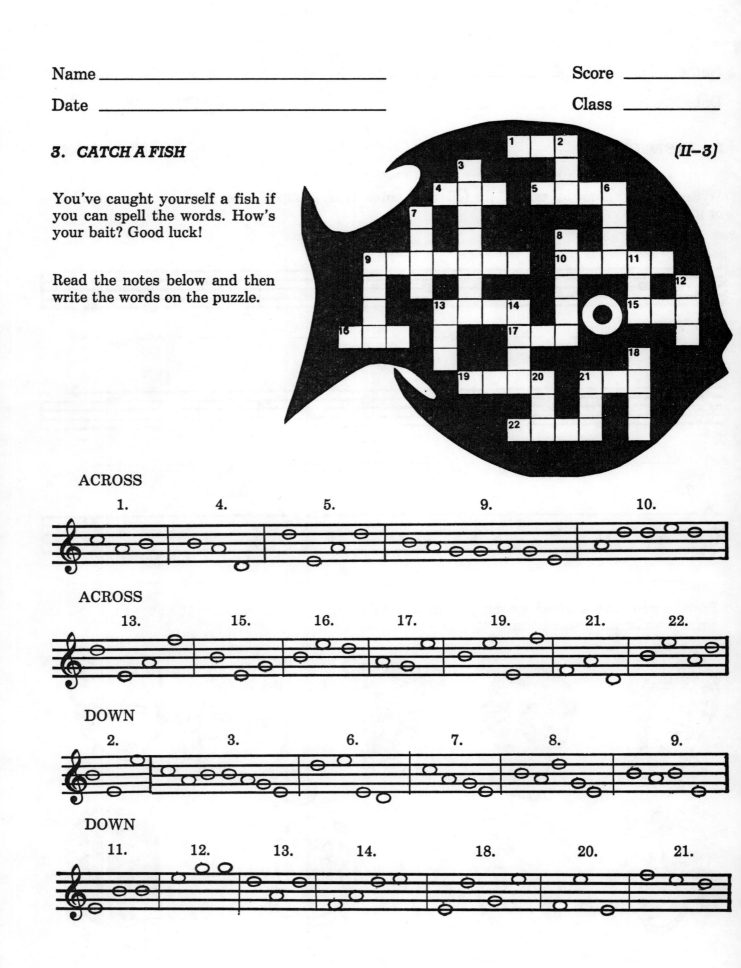

ACROSS

1.   4.   5.   9.   10.

ACROSS

13.   15.   16.   17.   19.   21.   22.

DOWN

2.   3.   6.   7.   8.   9.

DOWN

11.   12.   13.   14.   18.   20.   21.

4. COMPLETE THE STORY   (II—4)

Each group of notes spells a word. Use the words to fill in the blanks in the following story. The number "1" group spells the word for the number "1" blank, the number "2" group spells the word for the number "2" blank, and so on.

_____ (1) and her mom and _____ (2) were moving into a new home at the

_____ (3) of town. It was their last night in the old house. Everything was moved out except

a few boxes, a _____ (4), some _____ (5), and a sleeping _____ (6).

_____ (7) said, "It sure is _____ (8) around here." She _____ (9) to

have a party that last night, but _____ (10) said it was a _____ (11) time to

have friends over, and, too, it was late. Mom _____ (12) that there was no way she could

_____ (13) anyone, so a party was out. Just then the door flew open. There were Ruthie,

_____ (14) and _____ (15) standing in the doorway, yelling "Surprise!" Each car-

ried a _____ (16) filled with goodies. They also brought paper plates and cups. There was

even a jug of lemon _____ (17). What started out as a dull evening turned out to be a fun

time for all.

Name _____   Score _____

Date _____   Class _____

5. MUSICAL SPELLING   (II–5)

1. __ __   __ __   2. __   __ __   __ __   3. __   __ __   __ __   4. __ __   __   __   __

5. __ __   __   __   6. __   __   __ __   __   7. __   __ __   __ __   __   8. __ __   __ __   __ __

Write the letter names for the notes on the above spaces. Each group of notes spells a word, which may be new to you.

    Now read the following sentences carefully and use the above words to fill in the blanks. Use the dictionary if necessary. The above words will not be in the same order as in the sentences.

9. Jimmy said he was _____ out after running the race.

10. The class _____ farewell to the visiting foreign student.

11. The front or "face" of a building is called its _____.

12. After weathering many storms, the _____ tree finally fell.

13. "Haste makes waste" is a well-known _____.

14. A period of ten years is called a _____.

15. Land may be _____ from one country to another by treaty.

16. Using nails carelessly to hang pictures can _____ a wall.

Facade

Name _____   Score _____

Date _____   Class _____

6. CAN YOU NAME THEM?   (II-6)

The names of the following musical instruments are incomplete. The missing letters are from the Musical Alphabet. Write the missing letters on the blanks. Then draw the notes on the staff to match the letter names you wrote.

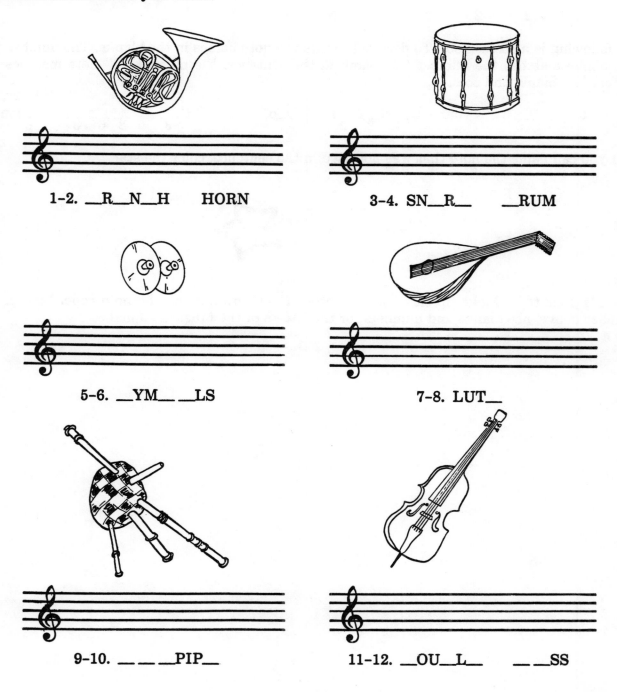

1-2. __R__N__H   HORN

3-4. SN__R__   __RUM

5-6. __YM__ __LS

7-8. LUT__

9-10. __ __ __PIP__

11-12. __OU__L__   __ __SS

7. READ A SECRET NOTE   (II–7)

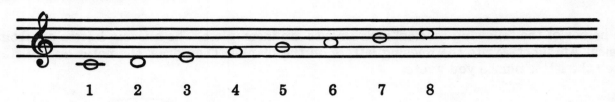

1   2   3   4   5   6   7   8

The following is a secret note. To decode it, write the note names in the blanks. The number "1" note above matches the number "1" blank in the sentence, the number "2" note matches the number "2" blank, and so on.

1. __on't   __ __ll   your   __ri__n__s;   __o   to   th__   __ __v__   __lon__.
    2   1 6   4 3 2   5   3   8 6 3   6 3

2. If you can name the note that was not used in the sentence, color the star.

??____??

Now it's your turn. Make up three secret notes of your own, using the note code. Like in the sentence above, use blanks and numbers for the letters of the Musical Alphabet.

3.

4.

5.

8. O.K., MESSAGE RECEIVED   (II–8)

Name the notes and then decode the sentences by writing the note names on the blanks. The order
of the notes matches the order of the blanks. These sentences tell what you should not do!

1.

2.   _o   _y   yours_l_   _or   _   _ip   in   th_   s_ _.

3.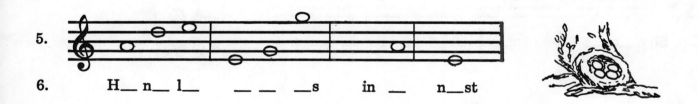

4.   Pi_k   _n_   _ _t   _ll   kin_s   o_   mushrooms.

5.

6.   H_ n_ l_   _ _ _s   in   _   n_st

7.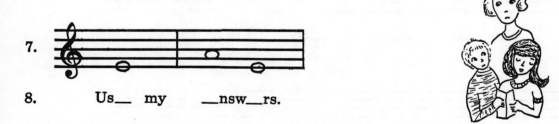

8.   Us_   my   _nsw_rs.

After decoding the sentences, rewrite them below with the words "Do not."

  9.
10.
11.
12.

Name _____   Score _____

Date _____   Class _____

9. MORE MESSAGES TO DECODE

Decode the secret messages by writing the note names in the blanks. The order of the notes matches the order of the blanks.

1. Th__ t__ __h__r w__nts to s__ __ you.

2. W__ __r__ __oin__ to __o__ __or __ppl __s.

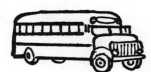

3. Som__on__ is m__kin__ __ __ __ __s.

4. W__ __r__ __oin __ hom__ __ __rly to __ __y.

5. Th__s__ m__ss__ __s __r__ __ll __ jok__.

This page could be called a "page of laughs." Why?

10. A CAGEY PROBLEM   (II–10)

Each group of notes spells a word. Write the letter names in the blanks for the missing words in the story.

Tom and Ann had a treehouse in their backyard. Their dog,

___ ___ ___ ___ (1), acted as watchdog, while ___ ___ ___ ___ (2), the cat,

napped in the treehouse. One day a ___ ___ ___ (3) came buzzing

around. ___ ___ ___ ___ (4) began to bark fiercely. ___ ___ ___ ___ ___ ___

(5), the bird, darted out of its ___ ___ ___ ___ (6), and ___ ___ ___ ___

(7) almost fell off the ___ ___ ___ ___ (8) of the treehouse. Tom

___ ___ ___ ___ ___ ___ (9) ___ ___ ___ ___ (10) and shouted, "You ___ ___ ___

(11) dog! Watch your business!" ___ ___ ___ ___ (12) paid no at-

tention to Tom and kept right on barking. In no time at all,

Ann had ___ ___ ___ ___ ___ ___ (13) back in her ___ ___ ___ ___ (14).

With all the commotion, how was she able to manage it? (Turn

page around for answer.)

Answer: No problem! Caddee's wings were clipped.

Name _____   Score _____

Date _____   Class _____

11. WHAT HAPPENS NEXT?   (II–11)

Write the missing words in the story by using the note names. Then
add a surprise ending on the back of this page. Your sentences should
contain at least three words using the Musical Alphabet.

Fall came quickly for Joan and her cousin, __ __ __. After spending two months in the moun-
                                              1

tains, the girls hated to leave. Joan and __ __ __ had fun planting a __ __ __ of vegetables. How-
                                            2   3

ever, as the summer __ __ __ __ __ __, only one lonely was __ __ __ __ __ __ __ __ __ left. __ __ __ felt
                          4   5   6

it had something to do with __ __ __ __ __, the little rabbit that Joan had tamed. "Look, he's 'snitched'
                                 7

so many carrots he's almost too fat for his __ __ __ __," said __ __ __. Defensively, Joan cried out,
                                               8   9

"Don't forget, he is my rabbit! You never did __ __ __ __ him, clean his __ __ __ __, or search in the
                                                 10   11

night for carrots. Oops . . ."

12. CROSSWORD PUZZLE

Each set of notes spells a word. Write the words in the puzzle by their matching numbers.

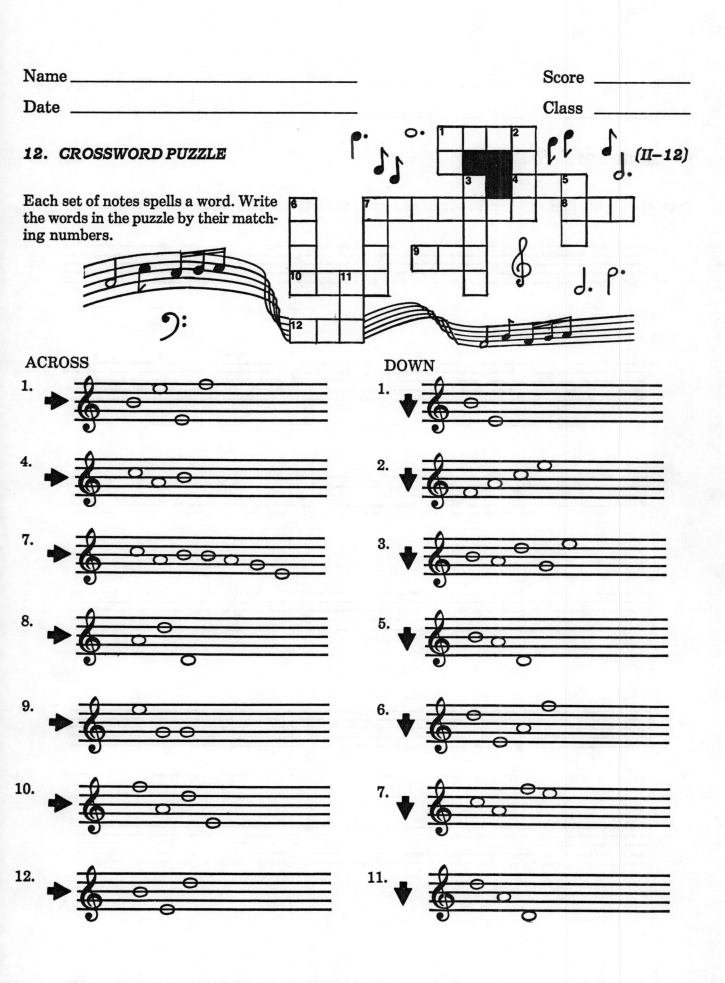

(II-12)

ACROSS

1.

4.

7.

8.

9.

10.

12.

DOWN

1.

2.

3.

5.

6.

7.

11.

13. MORE NOTES TO NAME

Draw the Treble Clef sign on the staffs and write the letter names below the notes.

Name_____   Score _____

Date _____   Class _____

14. SPELL THE WORDS   (II–14)

Each group of notes spells a word. Write the letter names of the notes on the blank under each group.

1._____ 2._____ 3._____ 4._____

5._____ 6._____ 7._____ 8._____

9._____ 10._____ 11._____ 12._____

13._____ 14._____ 15._____ 16._____

17._____ 18._____ 19._____ 20._____ 21._____

15. DRAWING NOTES   (II–15)

Draw the Treble Clef sign on the staffs and then draw the proper notes above the letter names.

1.   G   D   B   F   A   E   C   G

2.   A   E   G   B   D   F   A   C

3.   C   D   F   B   G   B   E   A

4.   E   G   C   D   A   B   C   F

5.   F   C   B   E   A   F   D   G

6.   G   B   D   F   C   E   A   D

16. LEARNING ABOUT THE KEYBOARD (II–16)

On the keyboard below, the white keys have the letter names of the Musical Alphabet. The seven letter names repeat over and over. For every eight keys or notes, there are two with the same name. The distance between them is called an OCTAVE.

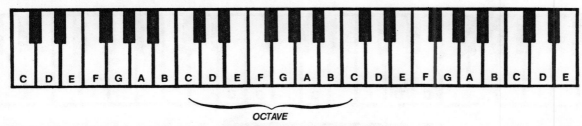

1. On the keyboard below, write the missing letters on the keys.
2. Draw the notes on the staff to match the letter names you wrote on the keys.
3. Label the notes. The beginning note is given. This note, called MIDDLE C, is found in the middle of the keyboard. In written music, it is on the leger line between the Treble and the Bass staffs.

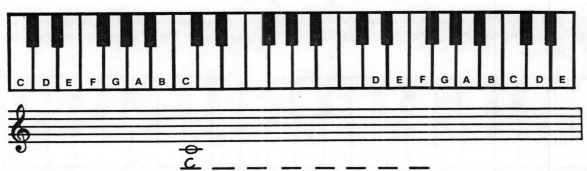

4. On the keyboard below, notice how the black keys are in groups of two and three. Circle each group of two black keys. Find each C, D, and E and write the names on the keys.

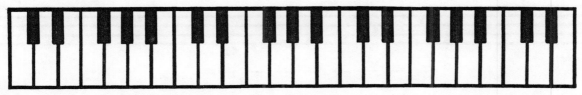

5. On the keyboard below, circle each group of three black keys. Find each F, G, A, and B. Write the names on the keys.

Name ______________________ Score ________

Date ______________________ Class ________

17. WRITE THE NAMES ***(II–17)***

1. When you sing or play the Musical Alphabet forward, each tone sounds higher than the one before. Write the letter names under the notes. The first one is given. Draw lines to connect the notes with the keys.

C D E F G A B C

C

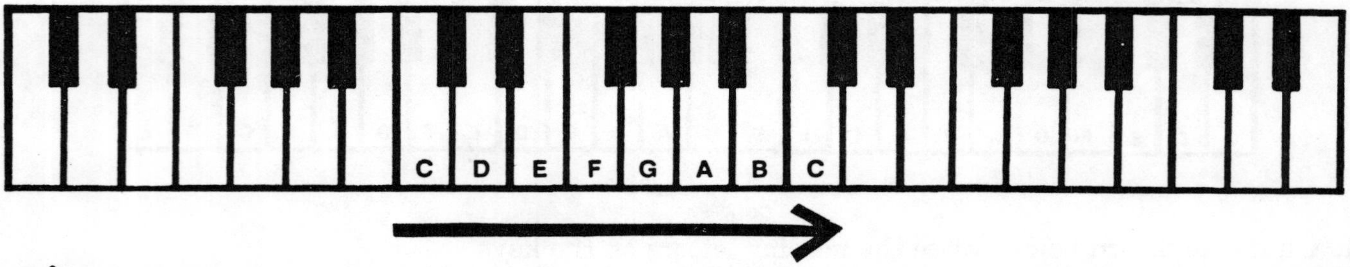

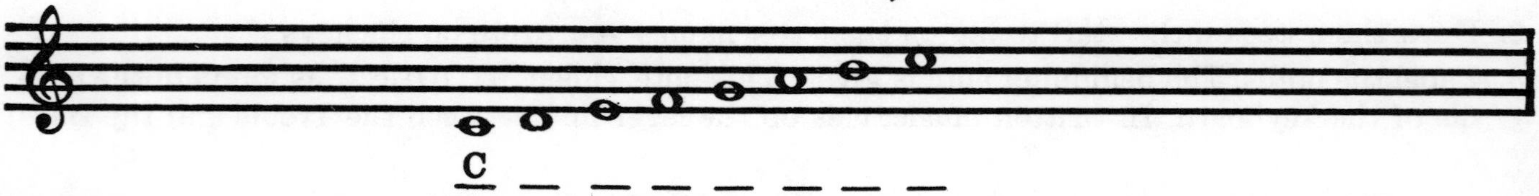

2. When you sing or play the Musical Alphabet in reverse (backwards), the tones sound lower. Write the letter names under the notes. The first one is given. Draw lines to connect the notes with the keys.

C D E F G A B C

C

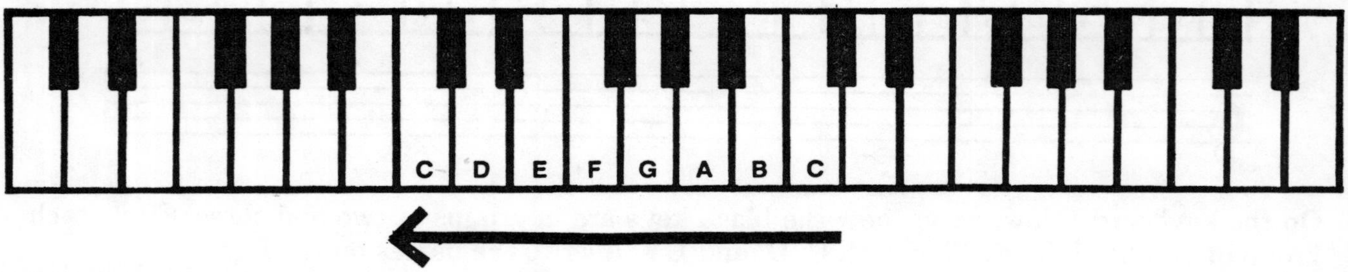

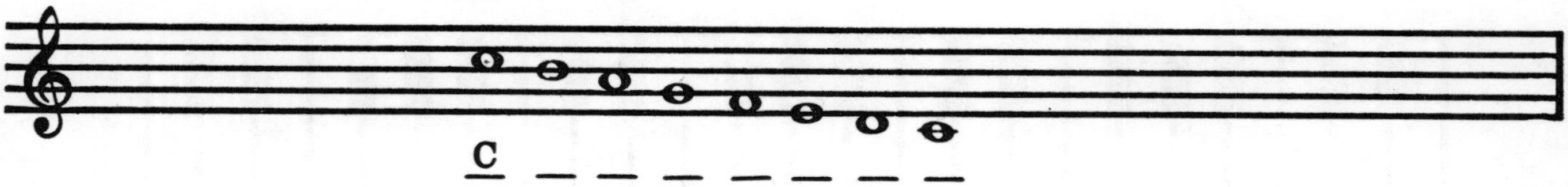

3. Write the letter name on each marked key.

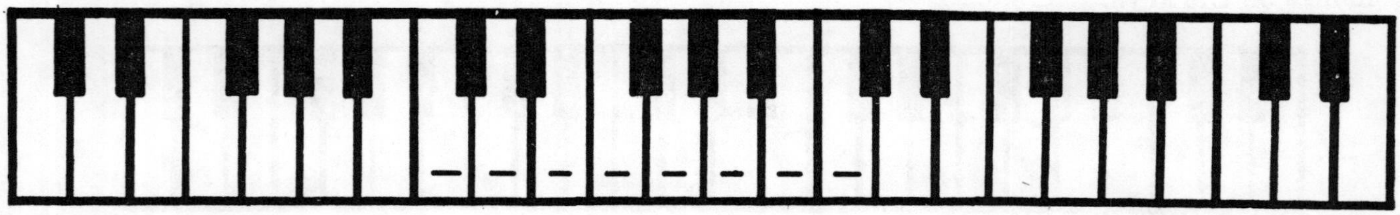

Name _____   Score _____

Date _____   Class _____

18. A MUSICAL MATCH   (II–18)

1. Study the example. Then write the letter names on each keyboard.
2. Match the keys to the notes with connecting lines.
3. Write the letter names of the notes. Each group of notes spells a word.

Example

F A C E

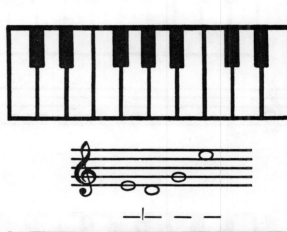

1. ___ ___ ___ ___

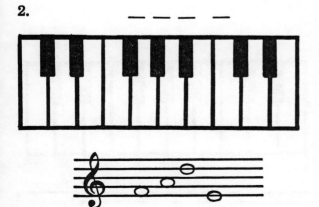

2. ___ ___ ___ ___

3. ___ ___ ___ ___

4. ___ ___ ___ ___

5. ___ ___ ___ ___

Name _____   Score _____

Date _____   Class _____

19. C FOR YOURSELF   (II–19)

Write the letter names of the notes on the keyboards. Each group of letters spells a word.

Name _____   Score _____

Date _____   Class _____

20. NOTE NAME PUZZLE

Use the letters of the Musical Alphabet. All the answers are one letter only.

Read each clue and write the answer in the matching square on the checkerboard. When you have finished, you will be able to check your work. The letters across the checkerboard will spell words, each row spelling a different word.

1. The added line between the treble staff and the bass staff is called MIDDLE _____.
2. Going up the scale, the note after G is _____.
3. The note between A and C is _____.
4. The bass clef is often called the _____ CLEF.
5. The orchestra will tune to this note. _____
6. The distance between Low C and High _____ is called an OCTAVE.
7. The lowest note on the treble staff is _____.
8. The first space on the treble staff is _____.
9. Complete the following musical pattern: CDE DEF _____FG.
10. The white key between the two black keys on the keyboard is _____.
11. The space note below the staff is _____.
12. Name the missing note: C D _____ F G A B C
13. The space notes spell F _____ C E.
14. The note on the fourth line on the treble staff is _____.
15. The names of the lines on the treble staff are: _____ G B D F
16. Name the missing note: C B A _____ F E D C
17. The space note on top of the treble staff is _____.
18. The white key to the left of the group of two black keys on the keyboard is _____.
19. The second space on the treble staff is _____.
20. The treble clef is often called the _____ CLEF.
21. Name the missing note: C B A G F _____ D C
22. The third line on the treble staff is called _____.
23. If "do" is C and "re" is D, what is "mi"? _____
24. What note comes next? C B A G F E_____

TEACHER'S GUIDE
AND ANSWER KEY

1. The Note Spelldown

    1. bead   2. face   3. dead   4. edge   5. gage   6. cafe

2. Pretending

    1. BAB   2. BEA   3. DEE

    4. DEB   5. ADA   6. ED

    7. GABE   8. BABE   9. ABE

3. Catch a Fish

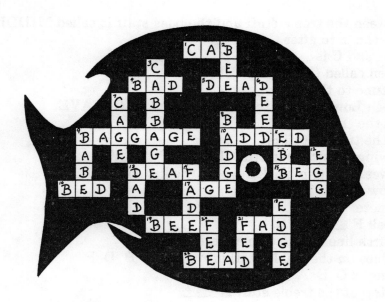

4. Complete the Story

1. Bebe	5. baggage	9. begged	13. feed
2. dad	6. bag	10. Dad	14. Fae
3. edge	7. Bebe	11. bad	15. Bea
4. bed	8. dead	12. added	16. bag
			17. ade

5. Musical Spelling

1. AGED	2. FACADE	3. DEFACE	4. ADAGE
5. BADE	6. CEDED	7. DECADE	8. FAGGED
9. fagged	10. bade	11. facade	12. aged
13. adage	14. decade	15. ceded	16. deface

6. Can You Name Them?

Suggest to students that they use notes from low C to high C for answers.

1-2. FRENCH HORN   3-4. SNARE DRUM   5-6. CYMBALS

7-8. LUTE   9-10. BAGPIPE   11-12. DOUBLE BASS

7. Read a Secret Note

Discuss what is meant by a code. Why are codes used? Explain the code that is used here. Point out that there are eight notes used. C is repeated. The notes start on C and end with C. That is called the C scale.

1. Don't call your friends; go to the cave alone.
2. B

8. O.K., Message Received

1. G B E F F A D E E A
2. Go by yourself for a dip in the sea.
3. C A D E A A D F
4. Pick and eat all kinds of mushrooms.
5. A D E E G G A E
6. Handle eggs in a nest.
7. E   A E
8. Use my answers.
9. Do not go by yourself for a dip in the sea.
10. Do not pick and eat all kinds of mushrooms.
11. Do not handle eggs in a nest.
12. Do not use my answers.

9. More Messages to Decode

1. The teacher wants to see you.
2. We are going to bob for apples.

3. Someone is making faces.
4. We are going home early today.
5. These messages are all a joke.

10. A Cagey Problem

1. Beag   2. Febe   3. bee   4. Beag   5. Caddee
6. cage   7. Febe   8. edge   9. faced   10. Beag
11. bad   12. Beag   13. Caddee   14. cage

11. What Happens Next?

1. Bea   2. Bea   3. bed   4. faded
5. cabbage   6. Bea   7. Baba   8. cage
9. Bea   10. feed   11. cage

12. Crossword Puzzle

13. More Notes to Name

1.   D   E   E   G   C   A   F   D
2.   B   F   E   G   B   A   B   E
3.   E   C   A   F   B   D   F   G
4.   A   F   D   C   G   A   G   B
5.   F   E   C   A   B   G   D   D
6.   A   B   D   E   F   G   G   E

14. Spell the Words

1. gadded   2. egg   3. baggage   4. bee
5. faded   6. ebb   7. deaf   8. cabbage
9. cage   10. bagged   11. faced   12. beef
13. cafe   14. adage   15. decade   16. gage
17. added   18. cab   19. dabbed   20. fed
21. add

15. Drawing Notes

Use the following staff as a guide to check the placement of notes. The lesson could be extended to use leger lines.

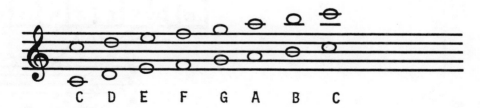

C D E F G A B C

16. Learning About the Keyboard

1.

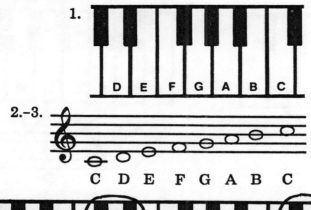

D E F G A B C

2.–3.

C D E F G A B C

4.

C D E   C D E   C D E   C D E

5.

F G A B   F G A B   F G A B

17. Write the Names

1.

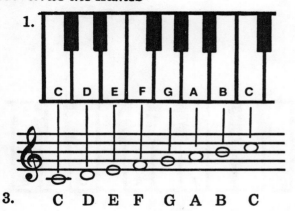

2.

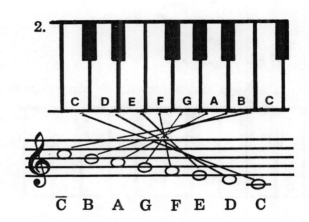

3. C D E F G A B C $\bar{C}$ B A G F E D C

18. A Musical Match

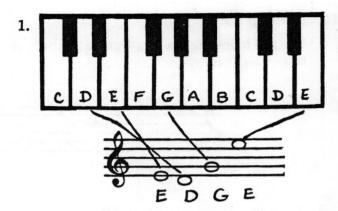

E D G E

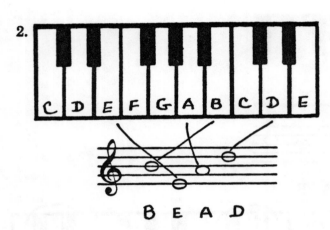

B E A D

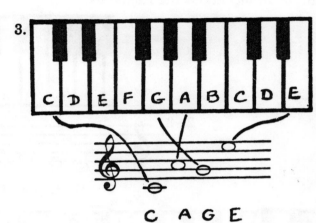

C A G E

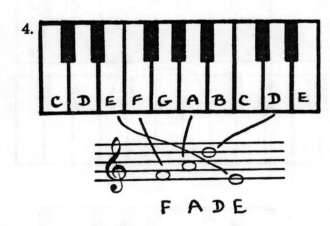

F A D E

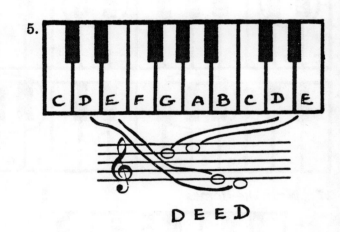

D E E D

19. C for Yourself

The keys and notes can be connected if desired.

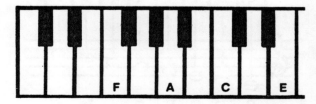

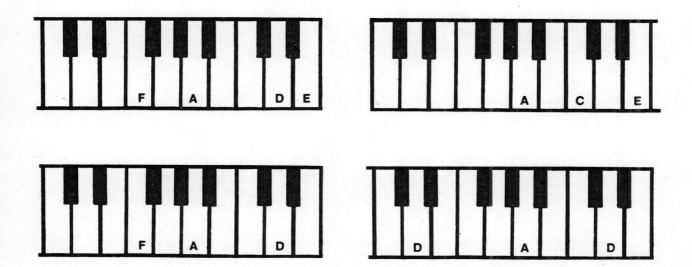

20. Note Name Puzzle

Before completing this lesson, students may need to be aware of this information:

(5): The orchestra tunes to the note A.

(23): One may use syllables to help measure the distance between one pitch and another. For example, the sound of the relationship do – mi is the same in all major and minor keys.

Scale Degrees: 1   2   3   4   5   6   7   8-1
             do re mi fa sol la ti do

Section III
RECOGNIZING PITCH DIRECTION USING DIFFERENT NOTES

No.	Activity Title	Skill Involved
1.	WHAT'S THE PITCH?	(Recognizing high and low notes on the staff)
2.	UP OR DOWN?	(Recognizing up and down on the keyboard)
3.	UP, DOWN OR REPEAT?	(Identifying up, down and repeat)
4.	LEARN MORE ABOUT NOTES	(Drawing quarter notes)
5.	TRY A TUNE	(Matching pitch levels with song titles)
6.	LEARN A RULE FOR STEMS	(Learning about stem direction)
7.	SHOW THE DIRECTION	(Analyzing pitch direction)
8.	NAME THE DIRECTION	(Recognizing pitch direction)
9.	PRACTICE WITH THE HALF NOTE	(Drawing half notes)
10.	NOTE THE CODE	(Drawing whole notes)
11.	FLAG THE NOTES	(Drawing eighth notes)
12.	THE MATTER OF STEMS—UP OR DOWN	(Deciding the direction of stems)
13.	WRITING MUSICAL PHRASES	(Composing two-measure-answer phrases)
14.	FIND THE SEQUENCE	(Sequencing numbers, letters and notes)
15.	CONTINUE THE SEQUENCE	(Circling the correct sequence)

TEACHER'S GUIDE AND ANSWER KEY

1. WHAT'S THE PITCH? (III–1)

Do you know what PITCH is? It is the highness or lowness of a tone. Musical sounds or tones are made by regular vibrations. PITCH results from the number of vibrations within a given time. The more vibrations there are per second, the higher the PITCH. The fewer the vibrations, the lower the PITCH is.

Notes show their pitch by where they are placed on the lines and spaces of the staff. See the first box below. Two notes are given. By comparing the notes as to pitch, we would say that the first note is low and the second note is high.

1. Complete the second box so it matches the first one. Write in the words "Low" and "High."

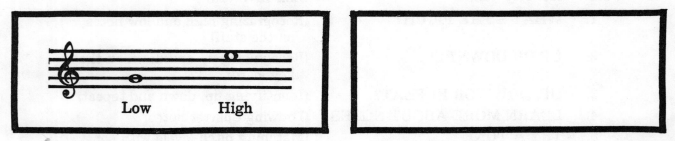

2. Each staff has two notes. One is placed high and the other low. In the given spaces, write "High" or "Low" as it applies to the note.

3. Draw two notes on each staff. Write "High" or "Low" as it applies to the note.

Name _____   Score _____

Date _____   Class _____

2. UP OR DOWN?   (III–2)

When keys are played from left to right, they go up or higher in pitch.
When keys are played from right to left, they go down or lower in pitch.

1. On the keyboard below, write the letter names of the keys between "Low C" and "High C." The
    letter name for "High C" and those above are identified by a line (C̄).

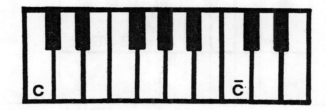

2. The following groups of letters are names of notes. When the keys are played, which direction
    does the pitch move? Show the pitch direction of the notes with an arrow. If the pitch moves up,
    point the arrow upward (   ). If the pitch moves down, point the arrow downward (   ).

    a. C D E ( )   b. B C̄ D̄ ( )   c. F E D ( )   d. A B C̄ ( )

    e. G F E ( )   f. D̄ C̄ B ( )   g. C̄ B A ( )   h. E F G ( )

    i. D E F ( )   j. E D C ( )   k. B A G ( )   l. A G F ( )

3. Write the letter names of the keys that are a step up from the keys named here.

4. Write the letter names of the keys that are a step down from the keys named here.

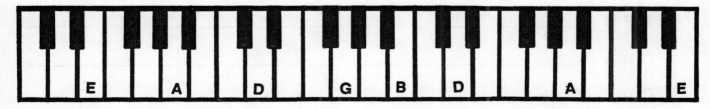

3. UP, DOWN, OR REPEAT?   (III–3)

To help you read notes, think by direction. Do the notes go up, down, or repeat (stay the same)? Examine the staff below the keyboard and notice that the lower notes are placed on the lower part of the staff and the higher notes on the higher part. The notes go up and down on the staff in the same order as they go up and down on the keyboard.

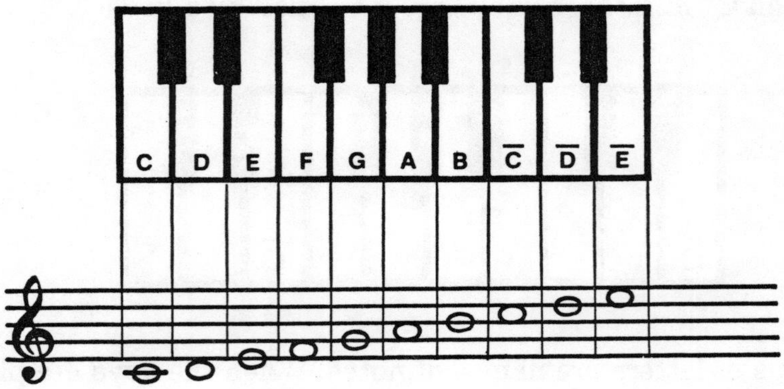

The following groups of letters are names of notes. Draw an arrow after each example to show which direction the notes are moving.

UP ↑   DOWN ↓   REPEAT →

1. C D E _____

2. C C C _____

3. A B C̄ _____

4. B A G _____

5. C D E F _____

6. G G G G _____

7. E F G A _____

8. C̄ B A G _____

9. C D E F G A _____

10. B B B B B B _____

11. C̄ B A G F E _____

12. F F F F   F F F F _____

Name _____   Score _____

Date _____   Class _____

4. LEARN MORE ABOUT NOTES   (III—4)

As we study "pitch," we see different kinds of notes. Some notes are filled in and others are not. We also see lines, called stems, connected to the notes. Some notes may have flags connected to the stems.

♩ is a QUARTER NOTE. The round part that is filled in is called the "note head." The line connected to it is called the "stem." It is about three spaces long.

1. Draw six Quarter Notes.

2. Draw a row of Quarter Notes as line notes. An example is given.

3. Draw a row of Quarter Notes as space notes. An example is given.

4. Stems on notes may also point down. These stems are connected on the left side of the notes. Draw a row of Quarter Notes with the stems pointing down. An example is given.

5. Draw a row of Quarter Notes as line notes with the stems pointing down.

6. Draw a row of Quarter Notes as space notes with the stems pointing down.

7. When a stem points up, it is connected on the _____ side of the note.

8. When a stem points down, it is connected on the _____ side of the note.

5. TRY A TUNE   (III–5)

Listed below are five well-known song titles. The beginning pitch levels for the songs are given in numbers. Match the pitch levels with the titles by writing the correct letters on the blanks.

_____1. "Mary Had a Little Lamb"
_____2. "Baa Baa Black Sheep"
_____3. "Row, Row, Row Your Boat"
_____4. "Are You Sleeping?"
_____5. "Yankee Doodle"

(A) 1 1   5 5   6 6 6 6   5   4 4   3 3   2 2   1

(O) 1 1   2 3   3   2 1   1 1   2 3   1   7   7

(L) 3   2   1   2   3 3 3   2 2 2   3   5 5

(G) 1   2 3   1 1   2   3   3   4 5   3   4 5   1

(R) 1 1 1   2 3 3   2   3   4 5

6. LEARN A RULE FOR STEMS   (III–6)

You have learned that stems can point either up or down. The basic rule is that stems point up (♩) on notes below the third line, and stems on notes above the third line point down (♩). On the third line stems can point either way. Generally, if the neighboring notes are lower, the stems point up, but if the neighboring notes are higher, the stems point down.

For each pair of boxes, fill in the second box so it matches the first one. Then complete the sentences at the bottom of the page.

When notes are written below the third line, the stems point up.

When notes are written above the third line, the stems point down.

On the third line, stems can point either up or down.

1. Notes written above the third line have their stems pointing _____.
2. Notes written below the third line have their stems pointing _____.
3. On the third line, stems usually point _____ if the neighboring notes are higher.
4. On the third line, stems usually point _____ if the neighboring notes are lower.

Name _____   Score _____

Date _____   Class _____

7. SHOW THE DIRECTION   (III–7)

Circle the correct answer for each of the following groups of notes to show which direction the notes are moving.

1. UP

   DOWN

   REPEAT

2. UP

   DOWN

   REPEAT

3. UP

   DOWN

   REPEAT

4. UP

   DOWN

   REPEAT

5. UP

   DOWN

   REPEAT

6. UP

   DOWN

   REPEAT

7. UP

   DOWN

   REPEAT

8. UP

   DOWN

   REPEAT

9. UP

   DOWN

   REPEAT

10. UP

    DOWN

    REPEAT

11. UP

    DOWN

    REPEAT

12. UP

    DOWN

    REPEAT

Name _____   Score _____

Date _____   Class _____

8. NAME THE DIRECTION   (III–8)

For each group of notes write the pitch direction (up, down, or repeat).
For numbers 10, 11 and 12, finish drawing the Quarter Notes by adding stems in the correct direction.

9. PRACTICE WITH THE HALF NOTE   (III–9)

♩ is a HALF NOTE. The head of the HALF NOTE is not filled in. Like the Quarter Note, it also has a stem. Remember, when the stem is pointed upward it is connected on the right side of the note.

1. Draw five Half Notes.

2. Draw a row of Half Notes as line notes.

3. Draw a row of Half Notes as space notes.

4. Draw a row of Half Notes as line notes with stems pointing down on the left side of the note.

5. Draw a row of Half Notes as space notes with stems pointing down.

6. Draw eight Half Notes as line notes using the code below. Check the stems to see that they are on the correct side pointing in the proper direction.

              U = Stem points up
              D = Stem points down

U   D   D   U   D   U   D   U   D

Name _____   Score _____

Date _____   Class _____

10. *NOTE THE CODE*   *(III–10)*

○ is a WHOLE NOTE. The head of the WHOLE NOTE is not filled in. Unlike the Quarter Note and Half Note, the WHOLE NOTE has no stem.

1. Draw five Whole Notes.

2. Draw a row of Whole Notes as line notes.

3. Draw a row of Whole Notes as space notes.

4. Use the Note Code below to complete the notes on the staff. Draw the stems and fill in the notes as necessary. Remember the rules for stems.

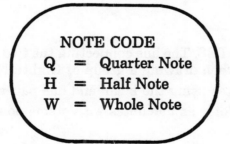

NOTE CODE
Q = Quarter Note
H = Half Note
W = Whole Note

Q   H   W   H   Q   W   H   W

11. *FLAG THE NOTES*   (III–11)

♪ is an EIGHTH NOTE. The head of the EIGHTH NOTE is filled in and a flag is attached to the stem.

1. Draw four Eighth Notes.
2. Draw a row of single Eighth Notes as line notes. Be sure to draw the flags on the right side. An example is given.

3. Draw a row of single Eighth Notes as space notes.

The same rules apply with Eighth Notes as with other notes that have stems. The stems that point up are connected to the notes on the right side and the stems that point down are connected on the left side. Notice that when the stem points down, the flag curves up on the right side like this: ♪

4. Draw two rows of Eighth Notes as shown by the examples.

♫ is a pair of EIGHTH NOTES. The line connecting the two notes is called a BEAM. Individual flags may also be used when drawing a group of Eighth Notes.

5. Draw one pair of Eighth Notes using the beam and one pair with individual flags.
6. Draw four pairs of Eighth Notes as line notes with stems pointing up.

7. Draw four pairs of Eighth Notes as space notes with stems pointing down.

Several Eighth Notes may be joined together like this: ♫♫

8. Draw four Eighth Notes connected with a beam.

12. THE MATTER OF STEMS—UP OR DOWN?   (III–12)

Decide in which direction the stems go and add them to these notes. The kind of note is written below each one. Fill in the note heads and add flags where needed.

1.

quarter   quarter   quarter   quarter   half   quarter   half

2.

eighth   eighth   eighth   eighth   quarter   half   quarter   quarter   half

3.

quarter   quarter   eighth   eighth   quarter   quarter   quarter   half   quarter

4.

quarter   eighth   eighth   quarter   quarter   quarter   quarter   half   quarter

13. WRITING MUSICAL PHRASES   (III–13)

A melody is divided into sentences just as words are phrased for speaking. These musical sentences are called PHRASES. Like sentences in a paragraph, phrases follow each other in music, and a question phrase may be followed by an answer phrase. While the question phrase ends on a note other than the keynote, the answer phrase will end on the keynote.

For the question phrase below, write a different answer phrase than the one above.

Make up two measure answer phrases to complete these phrases. Use the rhythm of the questions for your answers. Use the notes shown above the staffs.

Name ______________________________ Score __________

Date ______________________________ Class __________

14. FIND THE SEQUENCE *(III–14)*

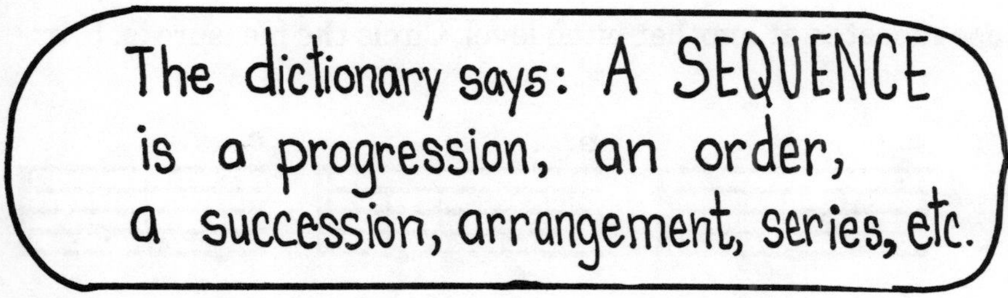

The dictionary says: A SEQUENCE is a progression, an order, a succession, arrangement, series, etc.

Dictionary

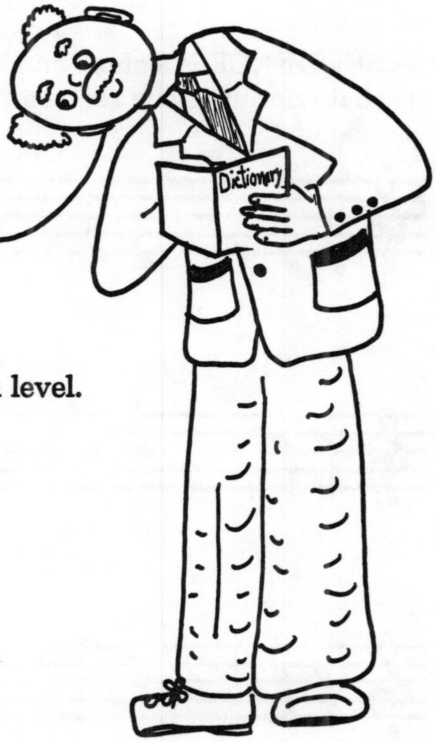

A SEQUENCE is a short musical phrase repeated at another pitch level.

Example:

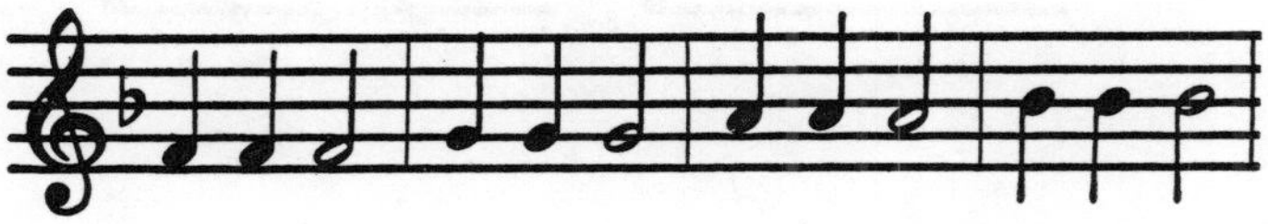

By using numbers, see if you can find the sequence. Write what comes next.

1.	**123**	**234**	**345**	**456**	______	**2.**	**246**	**357**	**468**	**579**	______
3.	**121**	**232**	**343**	**454**	______	**4.**	**4321**	**5432**	**6543**		______

MUSICAL ALPHABET

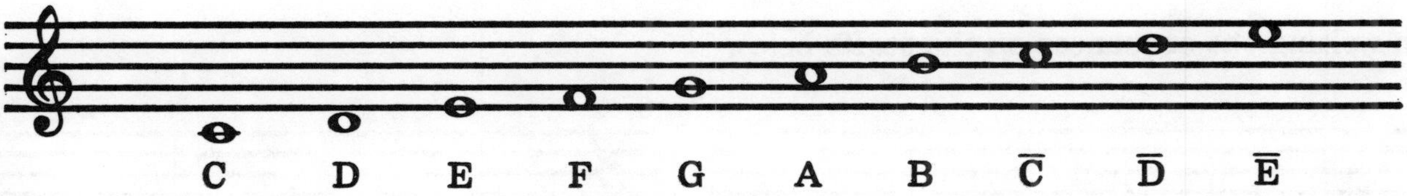

C D E F G A B $\overline{C}$ $\overline{D}$ $\overline{E}$

By using the Musical Alphabet, can you find the sequences? Write what comes next.

5. AAA BBB $\overline{CCC}$ ______ **6.** CCCC DDDD EEEE ______

7. ABA B$\overline{C}$B $\overline{CDC}$ ______ **8.** AAAB BBB$\overline{C}$ $\overline{CCCD}$ ______

9. $\overline{C}$B AG FE DC ______ **10.** CDEC DEFD EFGE ______

15. CONTINUE THE SEQUENCE   (III–15)

A SEQUENCE is a short musical phrase repeated at another pitch level. Circle the measure (a, b, or c) that continues the sequence.

Finish writing the sequences on the staffs below.

TEACHER'S GUIDE AND ANSWER KEY

(Section III)

1. What's the Pitch

1. Examples of answers are given.
2. High, low; low, high
3. Answers will vary.

* Suggest to students that they identify the letter names of notes.

2. Up or Down?

Play examples of notes going higher and lower on a keyboard instrument. Students can show with their hands how the melody moves up and down.

1. D E F G A B

2. (Direction of arrows are:)

a. up	b. up	c. down	d. up
e. down	f. down	g. down	h. up
i. up	j. down	k. down	l. down

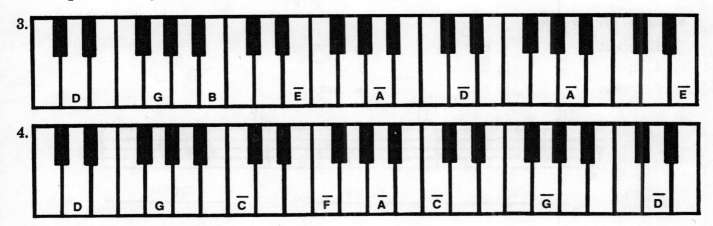

3.

4.

3. Up, Down, or Repeat?

Suggested game: Play notes going up, down, or repeated on a keyboard instrument. Without the other players seeing which direction the notes are being played, ask someone for the direction. If the answer is right, that player takes a turn.

1. up	5. up	9. up
2. repeat	6. repeat	10. same
3. up	7. up	11. down
4. down	8. down	12. same

* Identify groupings of three and four notes. Numbers 1 through 4 and 9 through 11 are in groups of three notes each. All others are in groupings of four notes.

4. *Learn More About Notes*

A quarter note receives one beat. Draw four quarter notes in a row on the chalkboard. Say "quarter" for each note. Use a drum for a steady beat. Students may clap or tap along with the steady beat. Examples of answers are given.

5. *Try a Tune*

1. __L__ 2. __A__ 3. __R__ 4. __G__ 5. __O__

* Define Largo (LAHR-go), meaning slowly and solemnly.

6. *Learn a Rule for Stems*

1. down
2. up
3. down
4. up

7. *Show the Direction*

1. up	2. repeat	3. down	4. up
5. repeat	6. down	7. up	8. down
9. down	10. up	11. repeat	12. down

* Draw a line under the notes with stems going up. Circle the notes with stems going down.

8. *Name the Direction*

1. repeat	2. down	3. down
4. up	5. down	6. up
7. repeat	8. up	9. down

* Write the letter names of the notes. Determine how many beats are in each measure. Write the Meter Signature after each treble clef sign. (Answer: $\frac{4}{4}$)

9. Practice With the Half Note

1.–5. Examples of answers are given.

6.

D D U D U D U D

10. Note the Code

1.–3. Examples of answers are given.

Q H W H Q W H W

11. Flag the Notes

Examples of answers are given.

12. The Matter of Stems—Up or Down?

1.

quarter quarter quarter quarter half quarter half

2.

eighth eighth eighth eighth quarter half quarter quarter half

3.

quarter quarter eighth eighth quarter quarter quarter half quarter

4.

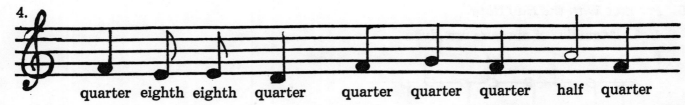

quarter   eighth   eighth   quarter   quarter   quarter   quarter   half   quarter

* Write the letter names of notes and add lines above high C. Add the Meter Signature at the beginning of the tune ($\frac{3}{4}$). Draw the bar lines. Write the Key Signature (Key of F) at the beginning of each staff.

13. *Writing Musical Phrases*

Listen to music with repeated phrases for students to respond to the end of each phrase by raising their hands. Phrases generally fall into regular groupings of four or eight measures.

A composer may use a little tune or phrase many times in a composition. The first phrase is always called "A." Any other phrases just like it are also called "A." The second phrase in the composition is called "B," and all others like it are called "B." If a third phrase is used, it is called "C." Analyze the given examples for students to determine the form.

If students have melody instruments to aid them in writing phrases, suggest they write phrases that will sound well. You may, however, tell your students that "anything goes." 1.-4. Answers will vary.

* Review Key Signatures: (1,2. Key of C Major   3. F Major   4. G Major)

14. *Find the Sequence*

1. 567   2. 6810
3. 565   4. 7654
5. $\overline{DDD}$ 6. FFFF
7. $\overline{DED}$ 8. $\overline{DDDE}$
9. BA   10. FGAF

15. *Continue the Sequence*

1. c   2. a   3. c   4. a

5.   6.

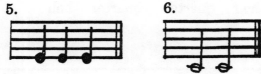

* Add Meter Signatures. (Numbers 1, 2, 4 and 5 are $\frac{3}{4}$. Numbers 3 and 6 are $\frac{4}{4}$.)

Section IV
FIGURING DURATION

TEACHER'S GUIDE AND ANSWER KEY

Name _____ Score _____

Date _____ Class _____

1. COUNT THE BEATS

To read music you need to know how long a note or tone is held. The length of time a note is held is called DURATION. Notes show duration by their shape and coloring.

The following chart lists five notes and their time values. In most music, a Whole Note lasts for four beats.

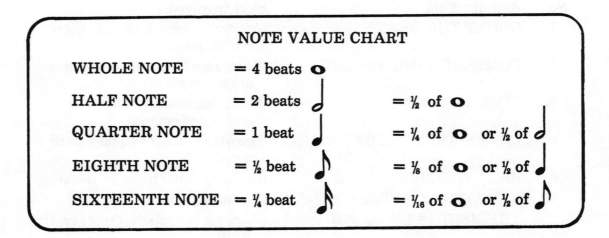

Use the Note Value Chart to answer the following:

1. The tone of a Whole Note lasts _____ times as long as the tone of a Quarter Note.

2. The tone of a Half Note lasts _____ as long as the tone of a Whole Note.

3. The tone of an Eighth Note lasts _____ as long as the tone of a Quarter Note.

4. The tone of a Whole Note lasts _____ times as long as the tone of a Sixteenth Note.

5. The tone of a Quarter Note lasts _____ as long as the tone of a Half Note.

6. An Eighth Note has _____ the beat value of a Whole Note.

Draw the following:

7. Two Half Notes = 1 Whole Note. ____ ____ = ____

8. Four Quarter Notes = 1 Whole Note. ____ ____ ____ ____ = ____

9. Eight Eighth Notes = 2 Half Notes. ____ ____ ____ ____ ____ ____ ____ ____ = ____ ____

10. Two Quarter Notes = 1 Half Note. ____ ____ = ____

Name _____   Score _____

Date _____   Class _____

2. COMPARE TIME VALUES   (IV–2)

Count to four for each group of notes in the chart. Then clap their time values aloud.

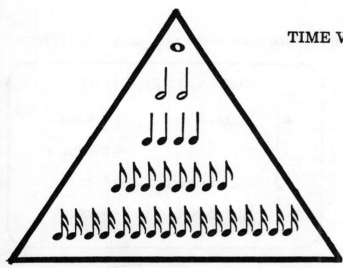

TIME VALUE CODE

If . . .
   1 Whole Note   = 4 counts
then
   1 Half Note   = 2 counts
then
   1 Quarter Note   = 1 count
then
   1 Eighth Note   = ½ count
then
   1 Sixteenth Note = ¼ count

Use the Time Value Code to fill in the blanks with the correct numbers.

1. One Whole Note sounds as long as ____ Half Notes.

2. One Whole Note sounds as long as ____ Quarter Notes.

3. One Whole Note sounds as long as ____ Eighth Notes.

4. One Whole Note sounds as long as ____ Sixteenth Notes.

5. One Half Note sounds as long as ____ Quarter Notes.

6. One Half Note sounds as long as ____ Eighth Notes.

7. One Quarter Note sounds as long as ____ Eighth Notes.

8. One Quarter Note sounds as long as ____ Sixteenth Notes.

Use the Code above to fill in the missing notes.

9. ♩ + __ = ♩   10. __ + __ = 𝅝

11. ♩ + __ = 𝅝   12. ♩ + ♩ + __ = 𝅝

Name _____

Date _____

3. TIME VALUES QUIZ

Any note sounds twice as long as the next note smaller in time value.

For example: 𝅝 = 𝅗𝅥 𝅗𝅥 , 𝅗𝅥 = ♩ ♩ , ♩ = ♪ ♪

Or, it takes two notes of the same kind to equal the time value of the next longer kind of note.

For example: 𝅗𝅥 𝅗𝅥 = 𝅝 , ♩ ♩ = 𝅗𝅥 , ♪ ♪ = ♩

TIME VALUES CHART		
𝅝	Whole Note	= 4 counts
𝅗𝅥	Half Note	= 2 counts
♩	Quarter Note	= 1 count
♪	Eighth Note	= ½ count

Use the Time Values Chart to answer the following.
Either draw the correct note or write the number of counts.

1. If 𝅝 = 4 counts then _____ = 2 counts.

2. If 𝅝 = 4 counts then _____ = 1 count.

3. If 𝅝 = 4 counts then _____ = ½ count.

4. If 𝅗𝅥 = 2 counts then _____ = 1 count.

5. If ♩ = 1 count then _____ = 2 counts.

6. If 𝅗𝅥 = 2 counts then _____ = 4 counts.

7. If ♪ = ½ count then _____ = 1 count.

8. If ♩ = 1 count then ♪ = _____ count(s).

9. If ♪ = ½ count then 𝅗𝅥 = _____ count(s).

10. If 𝅝 = 4 count then ♩ = _____ count(s).

Name _____   Score _____

Date _____   Class _____

4. LEARN ABOUT REST VALUES

There are places in the song where one does not sing or play. These silent beats are known as RESTS. Like notes, rests have time value. They may be found at the beginning of music or at the end. Sometimes rests occur between phrases of a melody. In a song, a rest may be used to allow the singer to take a breath.

Here are the symbols or signs and the names of the various rests. They are shown with the notes that equal them in time value.

Note		Rest		Beats
o	=	Whole Note Rest		= 4
♩	=	Half Note Rest		= 2
♩	=	Quarter Note Rest		= 1
♪	=	Eighth Note Rest		= ½

Draw four examples for each type of rest.

Whole Rests _____   Half Rests _____

Quarter Rests _____   Eighth Rests _____

After each note on the staff, draw its rest equivalent.

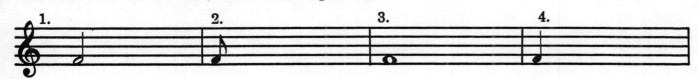

1.   2.   3.   4.

Name _____   Score _____

Date _____   Class _____

5. BALANCE THE SCALES   (IV–5)

Draw notes or rests on the right side of the scales to equal the value of the notes or rests on the left side. Notes can be balanced by other notes or rests, and rests can be balanced by other rests or notes. (Do not use the same symbol that is shown on the left side to balance the scale.)

Name _____   Score _____

Date _____   Class _____

6. KNOW YOUR NOTES   (IV–6)

Draw the correct note in the box to match the statement. Then name the note.

_____ 1. ☐   a note that is not filled in and has no stem

_____ 2. ☐   a note having one flag

_____ 3. ☐   a note that has a stem and is not filled in

_____ 4. ☐   a note that has a stem and is filled in

_____ 5. ☐   a note that sounds for 4 counts

_____ 6. ☐   a note that sounds for 2 counts

_____ 7. ☐   a note that sounds for 1 count

_____ 8. ☐   a note that sounds for ½ count

_____ 9. ☐   a note that is held twice as long as a Quarter Note

_____10. ☐   a note that is held twice as long as an Eighth Note

_____11. ☐   a note that is held twice as long as a Half Note

_____12. ☐   a note that has half the value of a Half Note

_____13. ☐   a note that has half the value of a Whole Note

_____14. ☐   a note that has half the value of a Quarter Note

7. THE REST IS UP TO YOU   (IV–7)

The composer of this song left out some rests in the music. A question mark is found below the staff for each rest that is missing. Write the missing rests on the proper places on the staff. You may use any of the following to complete the song.

WHOLE REST   HALF REST   QUARTER REST   EIGHTH REST

"The Rest Is Up to You"

by C. Morerests

8. PLAYING MUSICAL DOMINOS

(IV-8)

Here is the secret code to playing musical dominos.

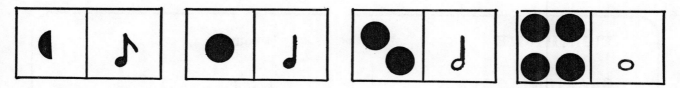

The left side of the domino represents the domino math. It is equal in duration to the note found on the right side.

Can you fill in the following dominos correctly so that both sides are equal in value? On each domino, write in the missing note or the correct number of dots.

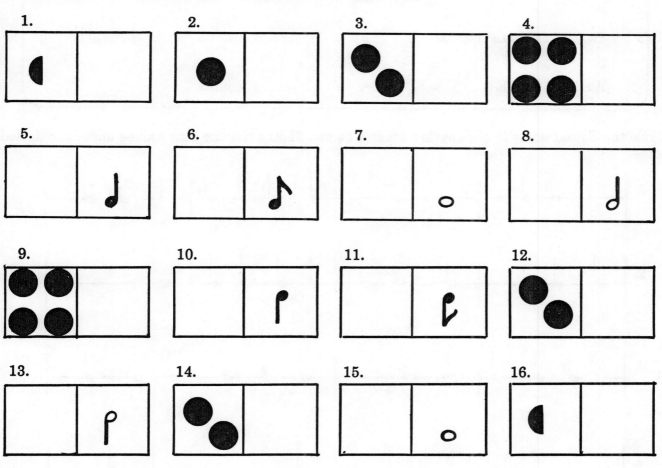

9. ADD A DOT

A DOT increases the value of a note by ½. A dot may be added to any kind of note to increase its value. A dot is added to the right of the note head as shown in the examples below.

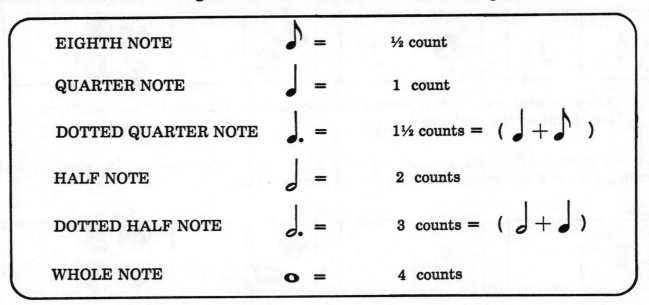

Circle the dotted notes in the rhythm studies below. Then write the time values under the dotted notes.

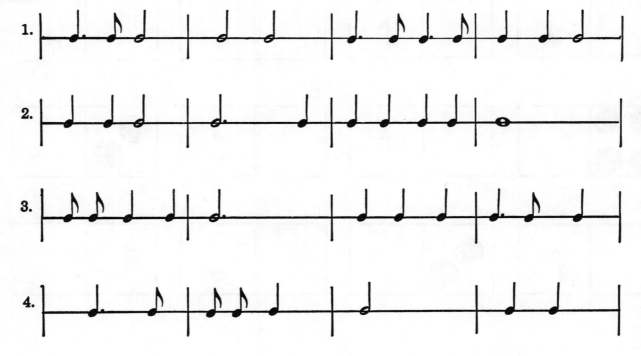

Name _____   Score _____

Date _____   Class _____

10. NOTE SEARCH   (IV–10)

Circle any two neighboring notes that equal the dotted notes below the note squares. The first one is started for you. The answers may appear vertically and diagonally, as well as horizontally.

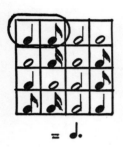

= 𝅗𝅥.

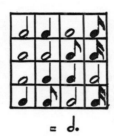

= 𝅗𝅥.

How many notes can you find in each?

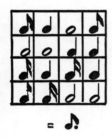

= ♪.

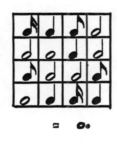

= 𝅝•

Can you figure out this puzzle?

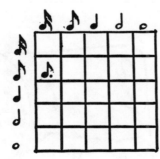

Where would you plot the dotted notes? The first answer is given for you in the puzzle.

Your answer will show a double line graph.

Name _____   Score _____

Date _____   Class _____

11. *MUSICAL MATH*   *(IV–11)*

Fill in the missing "addend" or "sum" by using one of these notes: 𝅝 𝅗𝅥 𝅘𝅥 𝅘𝅥𝅮

To check your answers, write the time value after each note. The first example is done for you.

1.	2.	3.	4.	5.
𝅗𝅥 = 2	𝅗𝅥	𝅘𝅥	𝅘𝅥𝅮	𝅗𝅥
𝅗𝅥 = 2	𝅗𝅥			𝅗𝅥
𝅝 = 4		𝅗𝅥	𝅘𝅥	

6.	7.	8.	9.	10.
𝅘𝅥	𝅘𝅥	𝅗𝅥	𝅗𝅥	𝅘𝅥𝅮
𝅘𝅥	𝅗𝅥	𝅘𝅥	𝅘𝅥	𝅘𝅥𝅮
𝅝	𝅝	𝅘𝅥	𝅝	𝅗𝅥

11.	12.	13.	14.	15.
𝅘𝅥	𝅘𝅥	𝅘𝅥𝅮	𝅘𝅥𝅮	𝅘𝅥
𝅘𝅥𝅮	𝅘𝅥𝅮	𝅘𝅥	𝅘𝅥𝅮	𝅘𝅥
𝅗𝅥	𝅘𝅥𝅮	𝅗𝅥	𝅘𝅥	𝅗𝅥

TEACHER'S GUIDE AND ANSWER KEY

1. Count the Beats

1. four
2. twice
3. half
4. sixteen
5. half
6. one eighth

7. 𝅗𝅥 𝅗𝅥 = 𝅝

8. ♩ ♩ ♩ ♩ = 𝅝

9. ♪♪♪♪♪♪♪♪ = 𝅗𝅥 𝅗𝅥

10. ♩ ♩ = 𝅗𝅥

2. Compare Time Values

The underlined numbers and symbols indicate where one should clap.

WHOLE NOTE	=	<u>1</u>		2		3		4		
HALF NOTE	=	<u>1</u>		2		<u>3</u>		4		
QUARTER NOTE	=	<u>1</u>		<u>2</u>		<u>3</u>		<u>4</u>		
QUARTER NOTE	=	<u>1</u>		<u>2</u>		<u>3</u>		<u>4</u>		
EIGHTH NOTE	=	<u>1</u>	<u>&</u>	<u>2</u>	<u>&</u>	<u>3</u>	<u>&</u>	<u>4</u>	<u>&</u>	
SIXTEENTH NOTE	=	<u>1</u> <u>e</u> <u>&</u> <u>da</u>		<u>2</u> <u>e</u> <u>&</u> <u>da</u>		<u>3</u> <u>e</u> <u>&</u> <u>da</u>		<u>4</u> <u>e</u> <u>&</u> <u>da</u>		

1. 2
2. 4
3. 8
4. 16

5. 2
6. 4
7. 2
8. 4

9. ♩
10. 𝅗𝅥

11. 𝅗𝅥 𝅗𝅥
12. ♩

3. Time Values Quiz

1. 𝅗𝅥
2. ♩
3. ♪
4. ♩

5. 𝅗𝅥
6. 𝅝
7. ♩
8. ½

9. 2
10. 1

73

4. Learn About Rest Values

Refer to the chart for answers 1–4. Ask students to think of ways they will remember the difference between the half and whole rest. For example, think of both rests as hats. Why would the hat worth four counts hang down from the line?

5. Balance the Scales

Answers will vary.

6. Know Your Notes

1. 𝅝 whole note
2. ♪ eighth note
3. ♩ half note
4. ♩ quarter note

5. 𝅝 whole note
6. ♩ half note
7. ♩ quarter note
8. ♪ eighth note

9. ♩ half note
10. ♩ quarter note
11. 𝅝 whole note
12. ♩ quarter note

13. ♩ half note
14. ♪ eighth note

7. The Rest Is Up to You

The question marks in the fourth measure of lines 2 and 4 use half rests. All remaining question marks use quarter rests.

8. Playing Musical Dominos

1. ♪
2. ♩
3. ♩
4. 𝅝

5. ●
6. ▮
7. ⠿
8. ⠆

9. ο
10. ●
11. ◖
12. ♩

13. ⠆
14. ♩
15. ⣿
16. ♪

9. Add a Dot

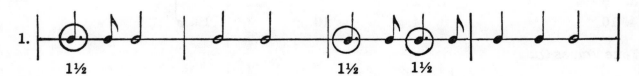

1½   1½   1½

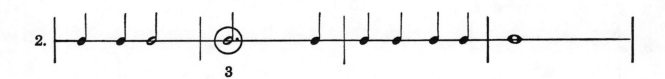

3

74

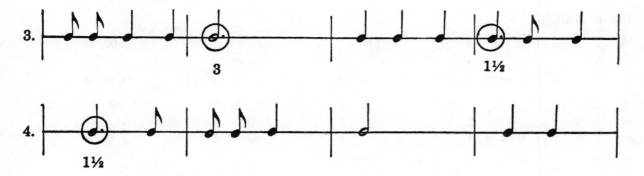

3.

3   1½

4.

1½

* Write the Meter Signature at the beginning of each line.
* Use as rhythmic patterns for melodic dictation.
* Play each line on a percussion instrument or on one key of a melody instrument.

10. *Note Search*

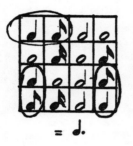

= 𝅗𝅥.

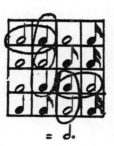

= 𝅗𝅥.

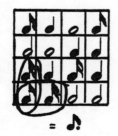

= ♪.

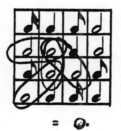

= 𝅝.

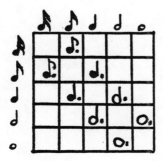

11. Musical Math

1. 2
   2
   —
   4

2. 𝅗𝅥 = 1
      1
      —
      2

3. ♩ = 1
      1
      —
      2

4. ♪ = ½
      ½
      —
      1

5. 𝅝 = 2
      2
      —
      4

6. 1
   1
   𝅗𝅥 = 2
   —
   4

7. 1
   2
   ♩ = 1
   —
   4

8. 2
   1
   1
   𝅝 = —
   4

9. 2
   1
   ♩ = 1
   —
   4

10. ½
    ½
    ♩ = 1
    —
    2

11. 1
    ½
    ♪ = ½
    —
    2

12. 1
    ½
    𝅗𝅥 = ½
    —
    2

13. ½
    1
    ♪ = ½
    —
    2

14. ½
    ½
    𝅗𝅥 = 1
    —
    2

15. 1
    2
    1
    𝅝 = —
    4

Section V
LOOKING AT METER SIGNATURES

No.	Activity Title	Skill Involved
16.	WHAT'S THE BOTTOM NUMBER?	(Writing the denominator for different Meter Signatures)
17.	DO THEY MEASURE UP?	(Completing measures with different meters)
18.	DRAW THE LINE	(Drawing bar lines to match rhythm with song titles)
19.	HELP THE ABSENT-MINDED COMPOSER	(Adding notes to complete measures)
20.	MATCH THE RHYTHM	(Matching beginning rhythms with song titles)
21.	FIND THE NOTE	(Examining units of measurement)
22.	BOX THE BEAT	(Recognizing which note gets one beat)
23.	MUSICAL DIVISION	(Adding bar lines for different meters)
24.	LESSON IN DIVISION	(Completing meter chart and conducting pattern)
25.	BEAT THE TIME	(Determining note values)
26.	WHICH IS DIFFERENT?	(Distinguishing different measures)
27.	A METER QUIZ	(Reviewing facts)

TEACHER'S GUIDE AND ANSWER KEY

Name _____   Score _____

Date _____   Class _____

1. ACCENT THE BEAT   (V–1)

In music, RHYTHM begins with the underlying beat. The BEAT is a regularly repeated pulse that measures the length of each tone. The following two series of dots are organized into rhythmic patterns. The dots represent strong and weak beats. Circle each group of beats.

1. • •

2. • •

The beat forms groups with an ACCENT (>) on the first beat of the group. This accented beat is called "1." Draw an accent mark (>) under the first beat in each group. The first one is done to show you how.

3. 1 2 3 1 2 3 1 2 3 1 2 3 1 2 3 1 2 3 1 2 3 1 2 3
    >

4. 1 2 1 2 1 2 1 2 1 2 1 2 1 2 1 2 1 2 1 2 1 2 1 2

Groups of beats that have a repeated accent are called MEASURES. The end of each measure is marked by a BAR LINE. A DOUBLE BAR is placed at the finish.

Measure   Bar Line   Double Bar

5. Draw an accent mark (>) under the first beat in each group of beats below.

1 2 3   1 2 3   1 2 3   1 2 3   1 2 3   1 2 3   1 2 3   1 2 3

Name _____   Score _____

Date _____   Class _____

2. *WRITE THE METER SIGNATURES*

When we study how notes should be arranged in a song, we think of METER. The word METER comes from the Greek word "metron" meaning MEASURE.

The two numbers that look like a fraction at the beginning of a song make up the METER SIGNATURE, also called the TIME SIGNATURE. The following are examples.

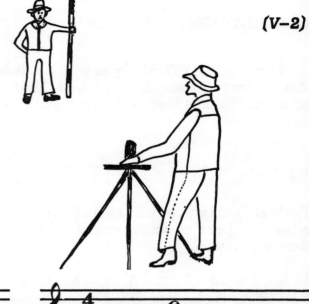

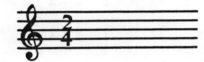 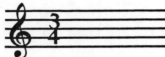 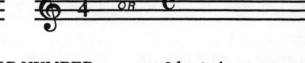

The Meter Signature tells how many beats or counts are in each measure and the kind of note that gets one count.

$\frac{3}{4}$ TOP NUMBER = 3 beats in a measure

BOTTOM NUMBER = the ♩ receives one count

The numbers of the Meter Signature are always written so that the third line on the staff comes between them. The Meter Signature is placed at the beginning of a piece of music. Unless there is a change of meter in the song, you will find the Meter Signature printed only once.

Read the statements below. Write the Meter Signatures on the staff lines to match the descriptions.

1. Three beats to a measure.
   Each Quarter Note gets one count.

   accented beats: strong weak weak

2. Four beats to a measure.
   Each Quarter Note gets one count.

   strong weak medium weak

3. Two beats to a measure.
   Each Quarter Note gets one count.

   strong weak

Name _____   Score _____

Date _____   Class _____

3. DOES IT MEASURE UP?   (V–3)

Below are the kinds of notes usually found in $\frac{4}{4}$, $\frac{3}{4}$ or $\frac{2}{4}$ time. Write the names of the notes and count their values.

NAME OF NOTE	NOTE	REST	TIME VALUE	METHOD OF COUNTING
1. _____	𝅝	▬	4 counts	
2. _____	𝅗𝅥	▬	2 counts	
3. _____	𝅘𝅥	𝄽	1 count	
4. _____	𝅘𝅥𝅮	𝄾	½ count	
5. _____	𝅘𝅥𝅯	𝄿	¼ count	

Remember, when reading the METER SIGNATURE . . .

6. 🎼 $\frac{3}{4}$ —the top number tells you how many _____ are in each measure.

7. 🎼 $\frac{3}{4}$ —the bottom number tells which kind of _____ gets one count or one beat.

Complete the melodies on this page by drawing bar lines to divide the groups of beats. Look at the top number of the Meter Signature to determine the number of beats in each measure. The first bar line is given.

8.

9.

10.

Name _____   Score _____

Date _____   Class _____

4. DRAW THE MATCHING NOTES   (V–4)

1. Complete the chart by adding the proper note, rest, and number of counts each gets.

	DRAW THE NOTE	DRAW THE REST	HOW MANY COUNTS?
WHOLE NOTE			
HALF NOTE			
QUARTER NOTE			
EIGHTH NOTE			

Write your answers in the blanks below.

2. The two numbers found at the beginning of a song are called the _____.

3. [time signature 4/4] —the top number tells you how many _____ there are in each measure.

4. [time signature 4/4] —the bottom number tells you which _____ gets one count or one beat.

This sign [C common time] means COMMON TIME. It means the same as [4/4] time.

5. Draw a Common Time sign after the clef sign on the staff below.

6. Rewrite the melody on the staff below the tune. Add the missing bar lines to match the Meter Signatures. Remember that the Meter Signature refers to the number of BEATS—NOT the number of NOTES in each measure.

Name _____

Date _____

Score Score _____

Class _____

5. WHAT'S THE TIME? (V-5)

When speaking of the Time or Meter Signature of a song, we may simply say the "meter." It tells you how many beats there are in each measure. The most common meters are: DUPLE METER (2/4), TRIPLE METER (3/4) and QUADRUPLE METER (4/4). These terms give a clue as to their meaning.

Write the number of beats in each measure for the three different meters.

1. Duple Meter = _____ beats per measure

2. Triple Meter = _____ beats per measure

3. Quadruple Meter = _____ beats per measure

Check your answers.   1. Two 2. Three 3. Four

The Meter Signatures are missing in the following measures. Write the Meter Signature after the Treble Clef sign in each example. Use either $\frac{4}{4}$, $\frac{3}{4}$, or $\frac{2}{4}$ time. The first one is done for you.

6. REWRITE THE SONG   (V–6)

Rewrite this song in $\frac{4}{4}$ time on the two bottom staff lines. The first measure is done for you. Can you name this tune? _____

7. DIP, DIP AND SWING   (V-7)

This song is missing the Bar Lines. Look at the Meter Signature.

1. How many counts are there in each measure? _____

2. Which kind of note gets one beat? _____

3. Add the Bar Lines and a Double Bar at the end of the song.

"Canoe Song"

Tradition Round

1. My pad- dles   keen and bright,   Flashing   with   sil-   ver
2. Dip, dip and   swing them back,   Flashing   with   sil-   ver

Follow the   wild goose flight,   Dip dip   and   swing.
Swift as the wild goose flight,   Dip dip   and   swing.

Drum accompaniment:

Name _____   Score _____

Date _____   Class _____

8. A METER QUIZ   (V–8)

When using these Meter Signatures, the note values are always the same.

$$\frac{4}{4} \quad \frac{3}{4} \quad \frac{2}{4} \quad \frac{5}{4} \quad \frac{6}{4}$$

1. What is the bottom number of these Meter Signatures? _____

2. What note does the bottom number stand for? _____

3. Draw the missing notes in the NOTE-REST CHART.

NOTE-REST CHART				
EIGHTH NOTE	_____ =	½ Count	= EIGHTH NOTE REST	𝄾
QUARTER NOTE	_____ =	1 Count	= QUARTER NOTE REST	𝄽
HALF NOTE	_____ =	2 Counts	= HALF NOTE REST	▬
WHOLE NOTE	_____ =	4 Counts	= WHOLE NOTE REST	▬

4. You can use many note and rest combinations to total 2 or 4 counts. Using the Note-Rest Chart, write a different combination with the counts underneath for each of the following. The first one is done for you.

♪ ♪ ♩ ♩ 𝄽	𝅝
½ + ½ + 1 + 1 + 1	= 4
	𝅝
	𝅝
	𝅝
	𝅝

	𝅗𝅥
	𝅗𝅥
	𝅗𝅥
	𝅗𝅥
	𝅗𝅥

9. BE A BETTER METER READER   (V-9)

The following music is written in $\frac{4}{4}$ meter. The first measure doesn't have the number of beats you would expect from this Meter Signature. A tune may start in the middle or the end of the first measure. When this happens, you should count the missing beats. They can be found in the last measure of the song.

Several notes are missing in this song. Study the Meter Signature and add the note that has the correct time value for that measure. The letter names of the missing notes are given under the staff. Draw the notes above the letters. The first one is done for you.

10. THE TREASURE HUNT

Join in the treasure hunt by finding the missing measures to "London Bridge" in the instruments below. Copy the measures in the correct order on the staff.

"London Bridge"

11. *UPBEAT VS. DOWNBEAT* (V-11)

Usually, melodies begin on the DOWNBEAT. Sometimes a melody begins on an "off" beat, a beat other than the first beat in the measure. Such a melody begins with an UPBEAT, often called a PICKUP. The words "down" and "up" refer to the conductor's hand—or hands—which move down on the strong beat, up on the weak beat.

A regular melody beginning on the first beat of the measure begins on the DOWNBEAT. When a melody begins with an UPBEAT, the missing beats are found in the last measure. When a song begins with an UPBEAT the total number of counts in the first and final measures will make a complete measure. The final measure is called an INCOMPLETE MEASURE. See the example below.

"A-Hunting We Will Go"

The top measure in the Meter Signature indicates the number of counts in each full measure of the song.

The beginning melodies below all begin with an Upbeat. Make up a final measure for each example. Write the number of counts for each note under the staff. (Remember, the combination of the first and last measures should equal the number of counts in each full measure.)

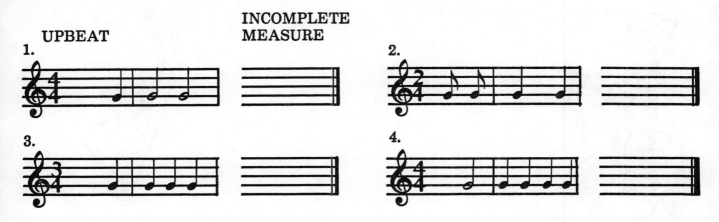

12. CHOOSE THE ANSWER   (V–12)

The Time Signature refers to the number of beats and not to the number of notes in each measure. Any number of notes and rests may be used in a measure, but they should add up to the number of beats indicated in the Time Signature. Notice how the rests and notes are combined to add up to the correct number of beats.

Study the music to answer the following questions. Underline the correct answer.

1. Which note receives one beat? (a.) Eighth Note   (b.) Quarter Note   (c.) Half Note

2. Which symbol tells us the rhythm? (a.) 𝄞   (b.) ♭   (c.) ¾

3. How many beats are there in the third measure? (a.) two   (b.) three   (c.) four

4. How many beats are there in the last measure? (a.) one   (b.) two   (c.) three

5. Which beat in ¾ time is accented?
   (a.) first   (b.) second   (c.) third

6. How many beats does the dotted Half Note receive?
   (a.) two   (b.) three   (c.) four

7. Which Rest is used?
   (a.) Half Rest   (b.) Quarter Rest   (c.) Eighth Rest

8. If you can figure out the name of this tune, write its title here.

   _____

Name _____   Score _____

Date _____   Class _____

13. FIND THE MEASURES   (V–13)

Look at the Meter Signature to decide how to divide this song. Draw bar lines and a double bar at the end.

"Tom Dooley"

Ballad

Hang down your head Tom Doo- ley,   Hang down your head and   cry.

Hang down your head Tom Doo- ley,   Poor boy, you're go-in' to   die.

Now answer these questions.

1. Number the measures for this tune. Write the numbers above the staff.

2. How many measures are in the song "Tom Dooley"? _____

3. Write the letter names under each note.

4. Circle the rest.

5. Name the rest. _____

6. Draw a block around the dotted note(s).

7. What type of notes are dotted? _____

8. Are there any measures repeated? _____ If so, which ones? _____

9. What does the double bar at the end of the second staff mean? _____

10. Which measure uses only a whole note? _____

11. Which measures use the rhythm: quarter, eighth, eighth, quarter, quarter?

_____

12. Write the Time Signature for the tune. _____

14. CROSS IT OUT

Music is sometimes written in COMPOUND METER: $\frac{6}{8}$, $\frac{9}{8}$ and $\frac{12}{8}$. The top number tells how many beats there are in a measure. The bottom number shows the eighth note (♪) gets one beat.

Below are the kinds of notes usually found in $\frac{6}{8}$, $\frac{9}{8}$ and $\frac{12}{8}$ time. Write the names of the notes in the spaces provided and count their values.

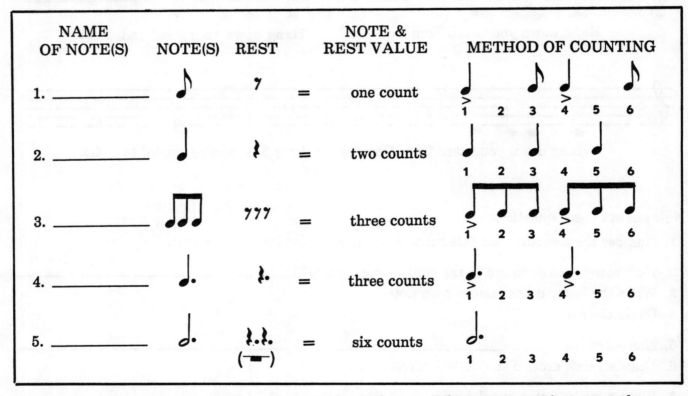

In the song below write the number of counts for each note. When a note receives more than one count, draw dashes between the numbers (1–2). The first measure is done to show you how. Several measures do not belong in the song. Cross out the measures which do not equal six counts. Can you name this familiar tune? _____

Name _____   Score _____

Date _____   Class _____

15. SUPPLY THE MISSING NOTES   (V–15)

Answer each question by filling in the blank. Draw the note and write its name.

1. In $\frac{4}{4}$ time the (   ) _____ note receives one beat.

2. In $\frac{3}{4}$ time the (   ) _____ note receives one beat.

3. In $\frac{2}{4}$ time the (   ) _____ note receives one beat.

4. In $\frac{6}{8}$ time the (   ) _____ note receives one beat.

5. In $\frac{3}{8}$ time the (   ) _____ note receives one beat.

6. In $\frac{9}{8}$ time the (   ) _____ note receives one beat.

Complete each measure using the correct number of notes that receive one beat each. The first two measures are done to show you how.

7. $\frac{4}{4}$

8. $\frac{3}{4}$

9. $\frac{2}{4}$

10. $\frac{6}{8}$

11. $\frac{3}{8}$

12. $\frac{9}{8}$

I'm a beat

I can be 1 beat, too

16. *WHAT'S THE BOTTOM NUMBER?*   (V–16)

If the top number of the Meter Signature tells you how many counts are in each measure, what does

the bottom number tell you? _____

_____

Draw the matching note in the brackets.

1. If the bottom number is 4, then a [   ] Quarter Note = 1 beat or 1 count.
2. If the bottom number is 8, then an [   ] Eighth Note   = 1 beat or 1 count.
3. If the bottom number is 2, then a [   ] Half Note   = 1 beat or 1 count.

Fill in the bottom number to match the note under the staff.

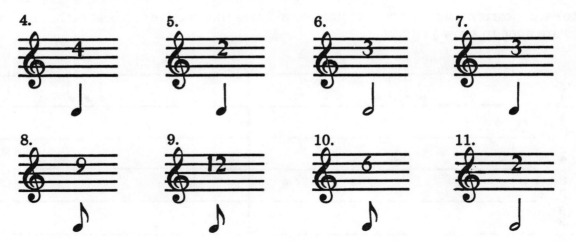

Study the measures below and fill in the bottom number for each Meter Signature.

Name _____   Score _____

Date _____   Class _____

17. DO THEY MEASURE UP?   (V-17)

$\frac{3}{4}$ TOP NUMBER   = Number of beats in each measure
                BOTTOM NUMBER = Kind of note that gets one beat

Answer the following questions by filling in the blanks.

1. $\frac{3}{4}$ How many (beats) in a measure? _____

    What kind of (note) gets one beat? _____

2. $\frac{4}{4}$ Beats? _____   3. $\frac{2}{2}$ Beats? _____

    Note? _____   Note? _____

4. $\frac{3}{8}$ Beats? _____   5. $\frac{2}{4}$ Beats? _____

    Note? _____   Note? _____

6. $\frac{6}{8}$ Beats? _____   7. $\frac{9}{8}$ Beats? _____

    Note? _____   Note? _____

The second measure in each example below is missing one note.

Draw a ♩ , 𝅗𝅥 or 𝅝 on the space "F" to complete the measures.

8.

9.

10.

11.

12.

13.

Name _____   Score _____

Date _____   Class _____

18. DRAW THE LINE

Draw the bar lines to divide these rhythms into measures.
The first measure is done for you.

The above rhythms belong to well-known songs. Their titles are listed below. Match the rhythms with the titles by writing the correct letter on the blank.

1. ____ "Twinkle Twinkle Little Star"

2. ____ "Old MacDonald Had a Farm"

3. ____ "Au Clair de la Lune"

4. ____ "My Country Tis of Thee" (America)

5. ____ "Merrily We Roll Along"

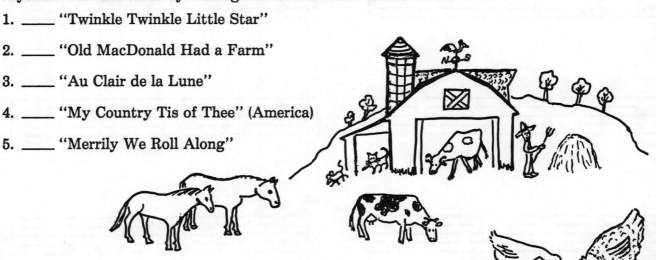

Name _____   Score _____

Date _____   Class _____

19. HELP THE ABSENT-MINDED COMPOSER   (V–19)

The composer of these phrases lost track of his counts, so one measure in each phrase is incomplete. Your job is to find that measure and supply the right number of notes so the counts correspond with the Meter Signature.

Name _____   Score _____

Date _____   Class _____

20. MATCH THE RHYTHM   (V–20)

Circle the rhythm pattern that is the best example of how each song begins.

1. "This Old Man"

     a.    **b.**    **c.**

2. "Bingo" (There Was a Farmer Had a Dog)

3. "The Star Spangled Banner"

4. "Are You Sleeping"

5. "America"

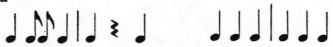      

6. "Three Blind Mice"

Name ______________________________ Score __________

Date ______________________________ Class __________

21. FIND THE NOTE *(V–21)*

Find the notes that receive one beat and circle them. Then find the notes that receive ½ beat and draw an "X" through them.

1. "America the Beautiful"

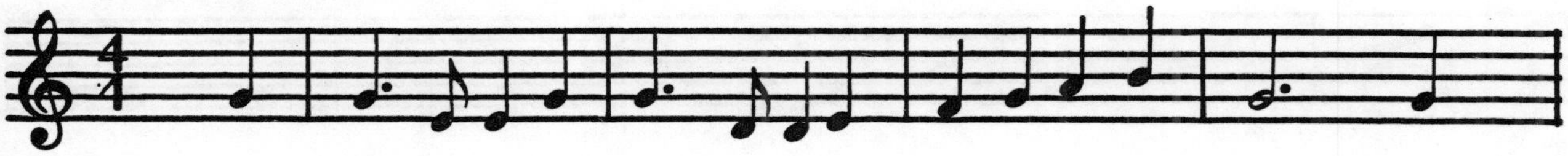

2. "Sing Together"

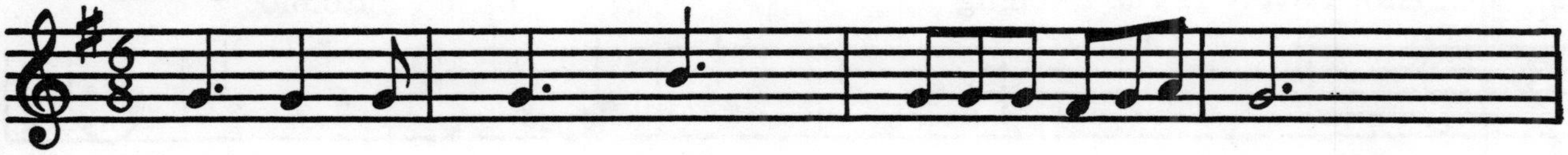

3. "There's a Hole in My Bucket"

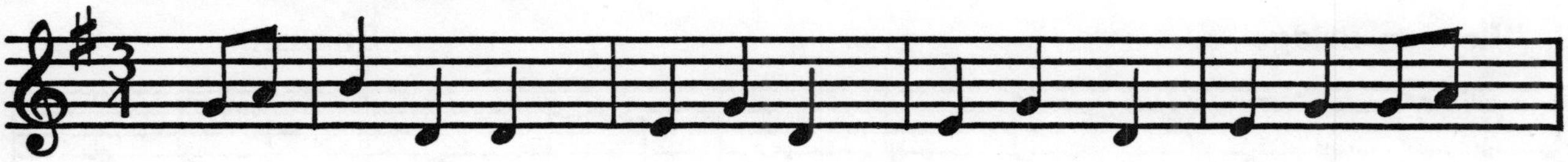

4. "Ol' Texas"

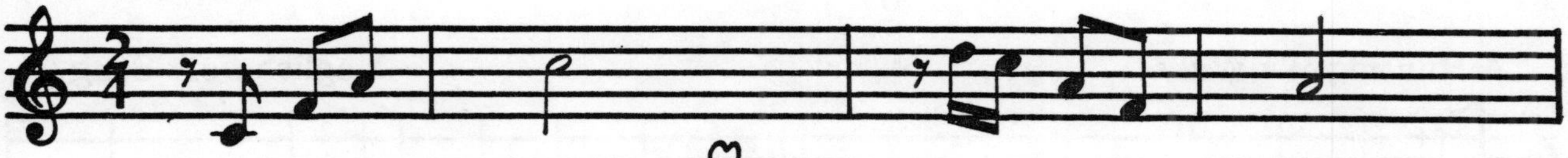

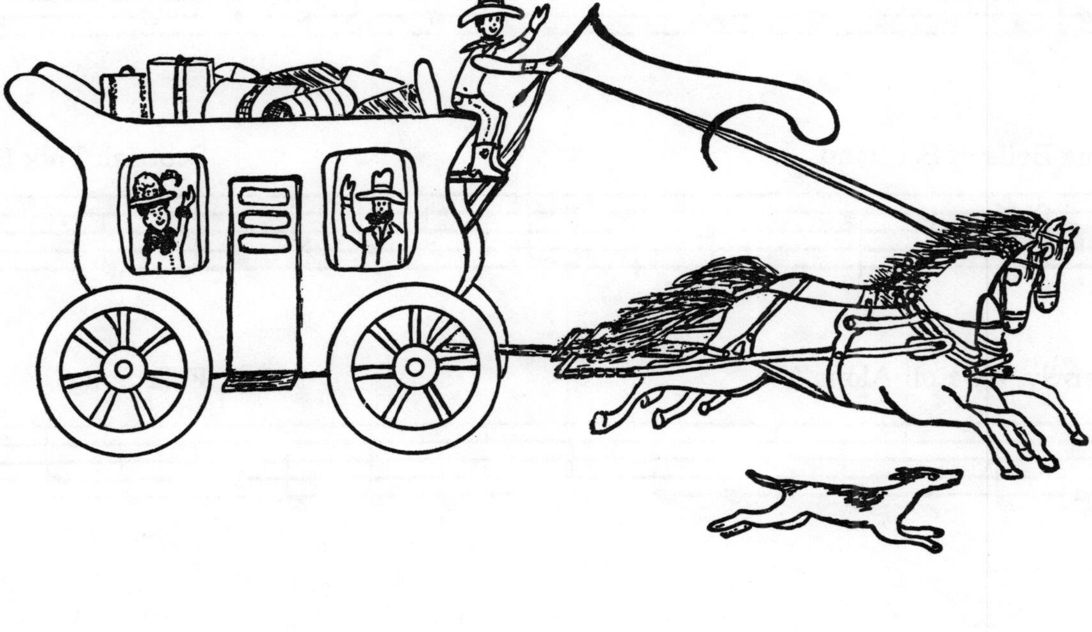

22. BOX THE BEAT   (V–22)

Look at the Time Signature at the beginning of each song. Draw a box around each note that receives one beat.

1. "The Star-Spangled Banner"   Francis Scott Key

2. "Oh, How Lovely Is the Evening"   Round

3. "London Bridge"   English

4. "A-Hunting We Will Go"   English Folk Song

5. "Blue Bells of Scotland"   Scottish Folk Song

6. "Merrily We Roll Along"   Folk Song

23. MUSICAL DIVISION   (V–23)

Draw bar lines to divide each line of music into measures.

1. $\frac{3}{4}$ ♩ ♩   ♩   ♩ ♩ 𝄾   ♩ 𝄾   ♩

2. $\frac{4}{4}$ ♩ ♩ ♩ 𝄾   ♩ ♩   ▬   ♩ 𝄾   ♩ ♩   𝅝

3. $\frac{2}{4}$ ♩ ♩ 𝄾   ♩ ▬   ♩ ♪ ♩ ♩ 𝄾   ♩

4. $\frac{3}{4}$ ♩ ♩ ♩   ♩ ♫   ▬ ♩ ♩ ♩ 𝄾   ♩.

5. $\frac{2}{4}$ ♫   ♪ ♪   ♫ 𝄾   ♩ ♩ ♪ ♪   ♫   ♪ ♪ ♪

6. $\frac{6}{8}$ ♫ ♫ ♫ ♫   ♩.   ♩.   ♫ ♫   ♩.   ♩ ♪ ♩ ♪

DANCING DIVISION

Name _____   Score _____

Date _____   Class _____

24. LESSON IN DIVISION   (V–24)

For each Meter Signature, draw the note that receives one count in the circle. Complete the middle part by drawing all the notes used with each Meter Signature. The longest held note for each meter is given. The first example is done to show you how. Can you see how this is a lesson in division?

NOTES USED WITH METER SIGNATURES

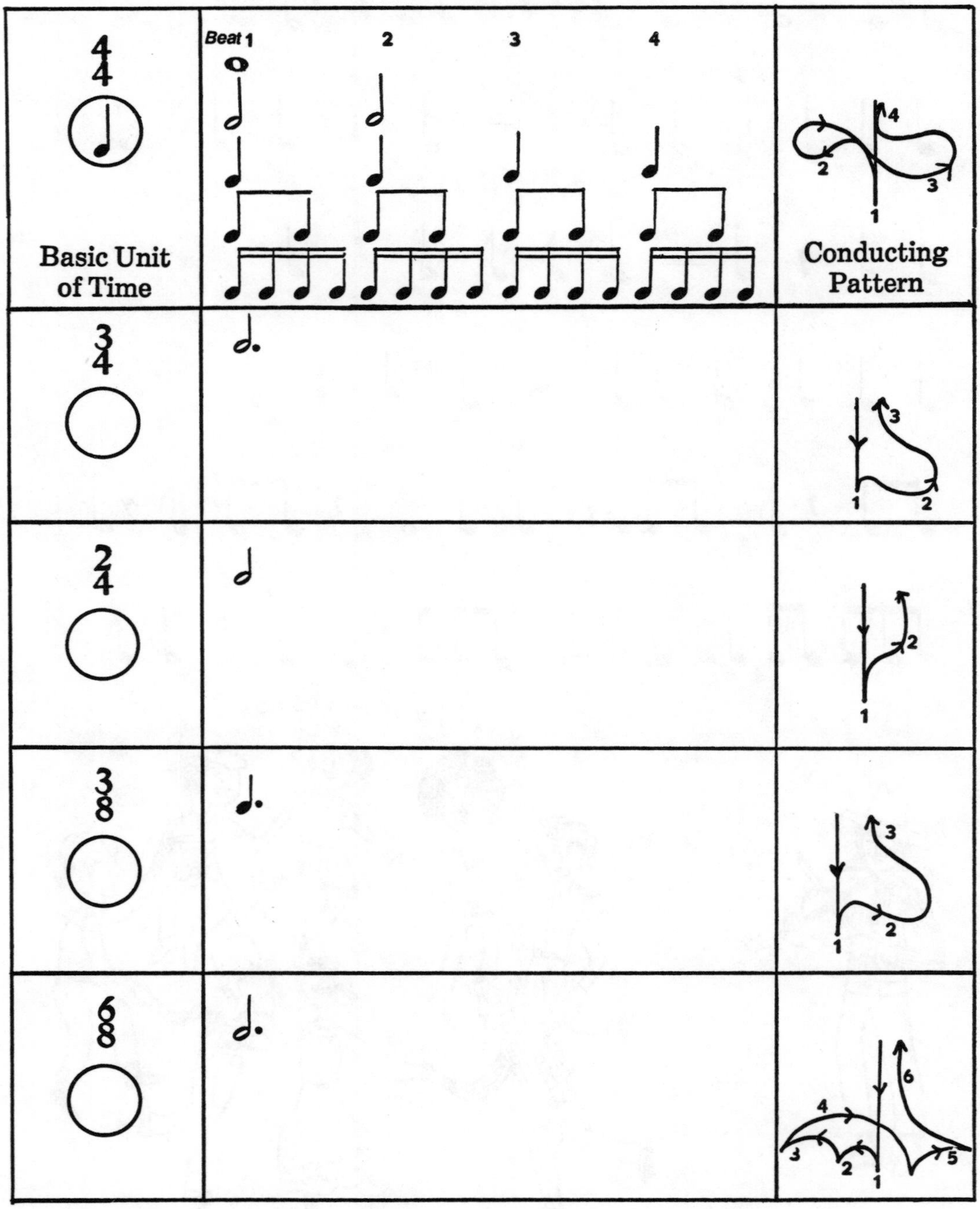

Name _____   Score _____

Date _____   Class _____

25. BEAT THE TIME   (V—25)

After you read the Time Signatures for the following songs, write the number of beats for each note. The first measure for both songs is done for you.

1. "I Know an Old Lady Who Swallowed a Fly"

I know an old la-dy who   swal-lowed a   fly,   I don't know why she

swal-lowed a   fly.   I   think   she'll   die.____

2. "Yankee Doodle"

Yank-ee Doo-dle   came to town a-   rid- ing on a   po - ny

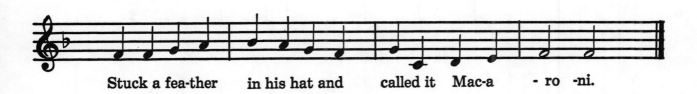

Stuck a fea-ther   in his hat and   called it Mac-a   - ro -ni.

Name ______________________________ Score __________

Date ______________________________ Class __________

26. WHICH IS DIFFERENT? ***(V–26)***

One measure of each line of music does not match the Meter Signature.
Draw an "X" through each incorrect measure.

a. b. c. d.

1. 2. 3. 4. 5. 6. 7. 8.

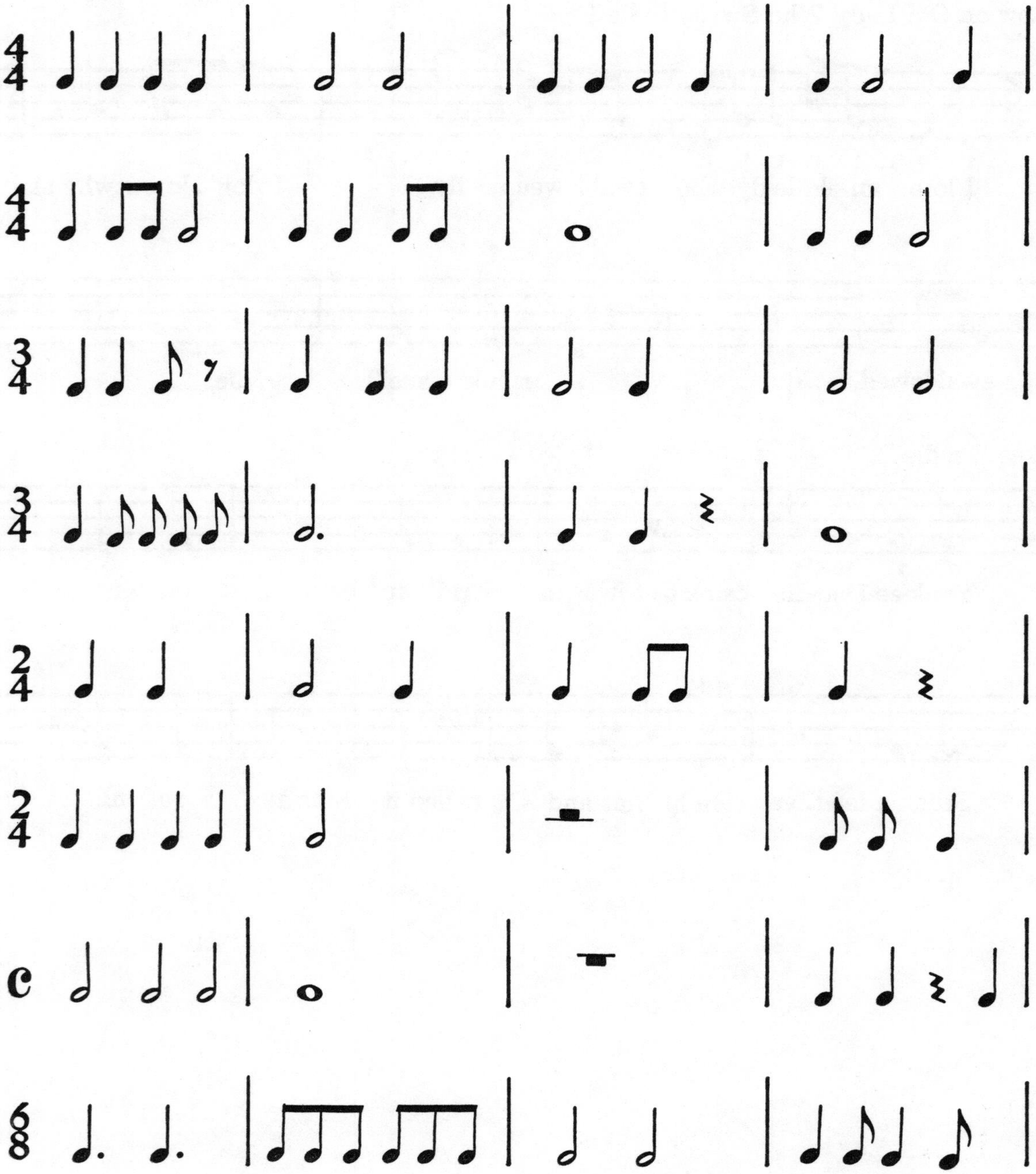

Name _____   Score _____

Date _____   Class _____

27. A METER QUIZ   (V–27)

Decide how many count(s) each note receives by looking at the Meter Signature. Write the number in the space provided.

.1 In $\frac{2}{4}$ meter the ♩ = ____ count(s).   5. In $\frac{4}{4}$ meter the 𝅝 = ____ count(s).

2. In $\frac{2}{4}$ meter the ♩ = ____ count(s).   6. In $\frac{4}{4}$ meter the 𝅗𝅥 = ____ count(s).

3. In $\frac{2}{4}$ meter the ♪ = ____ count(s).   7. In $\frac{4}{4}$ meter the ♩ = ____ count(s).

4. In $\frac{2}{4}$ meter the ♪ = ____ count(s).   8. In $\frac{4}{4}$ meter the ♪ = ____ count(s).

Use the Meter Signatures and Note Length Codes below to determine the number of counts each note gets. Write the time values under the notes. The first measure in each piece is done for you.

"Theme from Ninth Symphony"

Note Length Code   Ludwig van Beethoven

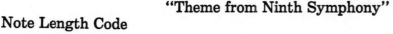

"The Arkansas Traveler"

Note Length Code   American

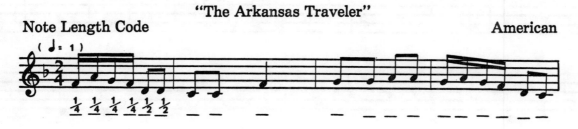

TEACHER'S GUIDE
AND ANSWER KEY

1. *Accent the Beat*

1. Each group of dots will be circled, for example:
2. Each group of dots will be circled, for example:
3. Each numeral 1 will have an accent mark drawn under it. |2 |2
4. Same as Question 3. |23 |23
5. The accent mark will be under each numeral 1.

2. *Write the Meter Signatures*

1. $\frac{3}{4}$ 2. $\frac{4}{4}$ 3. $\frac{2}{4}$

3. *Does It Measure Up?*

1. whole note
2. half note
3. quarter note
4. eighth note
5. sixteenth note
6. beats or counts
7. note
8.

9.

10.

* Play examples 8, 9 and 10 for ear training. Identify the titles.
8. "Hot Cross Buns"
9. "Twinkle, Twinkle Little Star"
10. "Pop Goes the Weasel"

4. *Draw the Matching Notes*

1. WHOLE NOTE	o	⊟	4 counts
HALF NOTE	♩	⊟	2 counts
QUARTER NOTE	♩	₹	1 count
EIGHTH NOTE	♪	𝄾	½ count

2. Meter Signature or Time Signature
3. beats or counts
4. note
5. 𝄴
6.

(Suggestions for questions 5 and 6.)
* Write the time values under each note.
* Write the letter names of the notes.
* Write the names for these beginning tunes. Answers: 5. "Yankee Doodle"
                                                        6. "London Bridge"

* Play the tunes.
* Finish notating the songs.

5. *What's the Time?*

1. Two	4. $\frac{2}{4}$	6. $\frac{2}{4}$	8. $\frac{3}{4}$	10. $\frac{4}{4}$
2. Three				
3. Four	5. $\frac{4}{4}$	7. $\frac{3}{4}$	9. $\frac{4}{4}$	11. $\frac{4}{4}$

* A student plays or claps rhythm for one of the examples while others guess which one it is.

6. *Rewrite the Song*

Title of song: "Skip to My Lou"

107

* Provide the students with words to the song to sing:

(chords) F

1. Lost my partner, what'll I do?   2. I'll get another, better than you!
    C₇   3. Flies in the butter-milk, shoo fly shoo!
   Lost my partner, what'll I do?   4. Little red wagon, painted blue.
    F   5. Flies in the sugar bowl, shoo fly shoo
   Lost my partner, what'll I do?   6. Cat's in the cream jar, ooh ooh ooh
    C₇   F   7. Off to Texas, two by two
   Skip to my Lou, my darling.   8. Lou lou, skip skip skip

* Sing the words to "Skip to My Lou." Mark the chords in the song for autoharp or guitar accompaniment.

7. *Dip, Dip and Swing*

1. 4
2. quarter

* Use the last measure of "Canoe Song" as a chant throughout, and as an introduction and coda.
* Sing as a round. The second group starts when the first group begins measure two.
* Use resonator bells E, G, and B for interesting effect to produce the e minor chord as an introduction or as an accompaniment.

8. *A Meter Quiz*

1. 4
2. quarter
3. eighth note

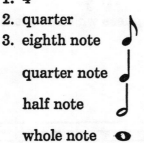

   quarter note

   half note

   whole note

4.

Notes	Equivalent	Math	Total
♪ ♪ ♩ ♩ 𝄽	𝅝	½ + ½ + 1 + 1 + 1	= 4
♩ ♩ 𝄽 ♩	𝅝	1 + 1 + 1 + 1	= 4
𝅗𝅥 ▬	𝅝	2 + 2	= 4
𝅗𝅥 ♩ 𝄽	𝅝	2 + 1 + 1	= 4
♪ 𝄾 ♪ 𝄾 𝅗𝅥	𝅝	1/2 + 1/2 + 1/2 + 1/2+2	= 4

Notes	Equivalent	Math	Total
♪ 𝄾 ♩	𝅗𝅥	1/2 + 1/2 + 1	= 2
♪ ♪ ♩	𝅗𝅥	1/2 + 1/2 + 1	= 2
𝄽 ♪ ♪	𝅗𝅥	1 + 1/2 + 1/2	= 2
♪ ♪ ♪ ♪	𝅗𝅥	1/2 + 1/2 + 1/2 + 1/2	= 2
♩ ♩	𝅗𝅥	1 + 1	= 2

9. Be a Better Meter Reader

1. C   D   C   2. E   D   C   G   C

3. D   A   E   C   F   4. A   C   E

* Form: ABA.
* Name the tune ("Oh Susanna"). The words and music are by Stephen Foster.
* Use autoharp or guitar accompaniment.
* Review dotted note values.

Chords: C   D₇   G₇

Chords: C   D$_7$ G$_7$

Verse —I came from Alabama with a banjo on my knee.

            C   G$_7$ C

I'm goin' to Lou' siana. My true love for to see.

            C   D$_7$ G$_7$

It rained all night the day I left the weather it was dry.

            C   G$_7$ C

The sun so hot I froze to death Susanna don't you cry.

           F   C

Chorus—Oh Susanna, Oh don't you cry for me.

            C   G$_7$ C

I came from Alabama with a banjo on my knee.

10. The Treasure Hunt

For children with little experience in reading and writing music, you may want to ask the following questions: "Locate the first measure. (It's the one with the treble clef and the time signature.) Ask them how they know the fifth measure. (It has a clef sign.) How can they find the last measure?

* Compare this variation of "London Bridge" with the one on activity page V-4.

11. Upbeat Vs. Downbeat

Answers will vary for incomplete measures.

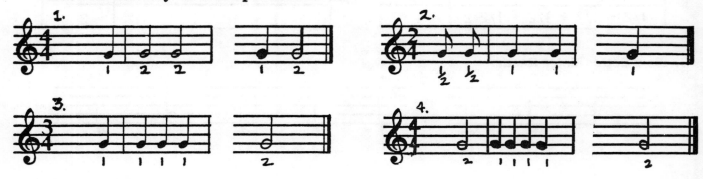

12. Choose the Answer

1. b   5. a
2. c   6. b
3. b   7. b
4. c   8. "Mexican Clapping Song"

* Clap on beats 2 and 3 of measures 4, 8, 12 and 16.

13. Find the Measures

1.

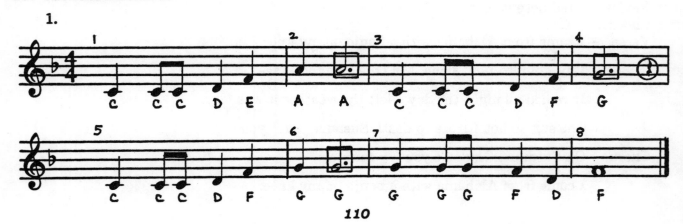

110

2. 8

5. Quarter note rest

7. Half

8. Yes, 1 and 3 are the same as 5

9. The end of the song

10. Measure 8

11. 1, 3, 5, 7

12. $\frac{4}{4}$

* Introduce SYNCOPATION (the placing of an accent on a normally weak beat).
* Review dotted notes.

14. *Cross It Out*

1. eighth

2. quarter

3. eighth

4. dotted quarter

5. dotted half

Name of tune is "Row, Row, Row Your Boat."

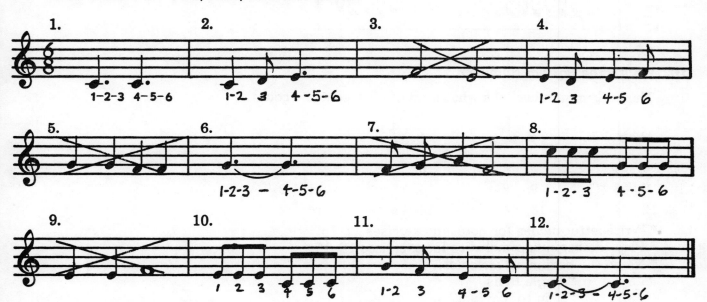

* Review TIE (a curved line connecting notes of the same pitch).
* Draw a TIE connecting notes in measure 6 and measure 12.
* Write the words for the song, lining them up directly under the corresponding notes.
* Clap and count note values to this song.
* Use "Row, Row, Row Your Boat" as a round to sing or play.

        1   2

Row, Row, Row Your Boat, Gently down the stream.

Merrily, merrily, merrily, merrily, Life is but a dream.

15. *Supply the Missing Notes*

1. quarter

2. quarter

3. quarter

4. eighth

5. eighth
6. eighth

7. $\frac{4}{4}$ ♩ ♩ ♩ ♩ | ♩ ♩ ♩ ♩ |

8. $\frac{3}{4}$ ♩ ♩ ♩ | ♩ ♩ ♩ |

9. $\frac{2}{4}$ ♩ ♩ | ♩ ♩ |

10. $\frac{6}{8}$ ♪ ♪ ♪ ♪ ♪ ♪ | ♪ ♪ ♪ ♪ ♪ ♪ |

11. $\frac{3}{8}$ ♪ ♪ ♪ | ♪ ♪ ♪ |

12. $\frac{9}{8}$ ♪ ♪ ♪ ♪ ♪ ♪ ♪ ♪ ♪ | ♪ ♪ ♪ ♪ ♪ ♪ ♪ ♪ ♪ |

16. What's the Bottom Number?

The bottom number tells what kind of note gets one count.

1. ♩   2. ♪   3. ♩ (half note)

4. 4	5. 4	6. 2	7. 4
8. 8	9. 8	10. 8	11. 2
12. 4	13. 4	14. 4	15. 8

* Write letter names for notes in exercises 12–15.
* Play the beginning melodies for exercises 12–15.
* Name the beginning melodies:
       "Jingle Bells"
       "Skip to My Lou"
       "Mexican Clapping Song"
       "Three Blind Mice" or "Hot Cross Buns"

17. Do They Measure Up?

1. 3, quarter   2. 4, quarter   3. 2, half   4. 3, eighth
5. 2, quarter   6. 6, eighth   7. 9, eighth   8. ♩ (half note)

9. ♩   10. ♩ (half note)   11. 𝅝   12. 𝅝

13. ♩

112

18. *Draw the Line*

1. T   2. E   3. M   4. P   5. O

* Define TEMPO (rate of speed at which music moves).
* Tap out the beginning rhythm patterns for songs while students decide which one they are hearing.

19. *Help the Absent-Minded Composer*

1. b   2. d   3. b   4. b   5. a   6. b

20. *Match the Rhythm*

1. b   2. a   3. a   4. c   5. c   6. b

* Play the correct rhythm patterns on a percussion instrument.

21. *Find the Note*

* Play these beginning melodies for students to become familiar with note values.
* Play melodies again in different order while students decide which melody is being played.
* Perform melodies on rhythm sticks while students decide which one they hear.

113

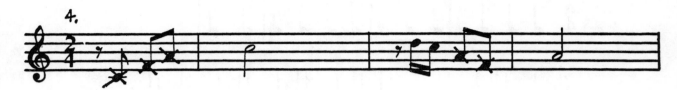

22. *Box the Beat*

* Write the note values under each note.
* Write the letter names under each note being sure to include accidentals.
* Play songs on a percussion instrument or melody instrument in a different order than shown for students to decide which one they hear.

1. "The Star-Spangled Banner"   Francis Scott Key

2. "Oh, How Lovely Is the Evening"   Round

3. "London Bridge"   English

4. "A-Hunting We Will Go"   English Folk Song

5. "Blue Bells of Scotland"   Scottish Folk Song

6. "Merrily We Roll Along"

23. Musical Division

* Clap the rhythm patterns.

24. Lesson in Division

* Play an example of music for each meter to let children experience conducting.

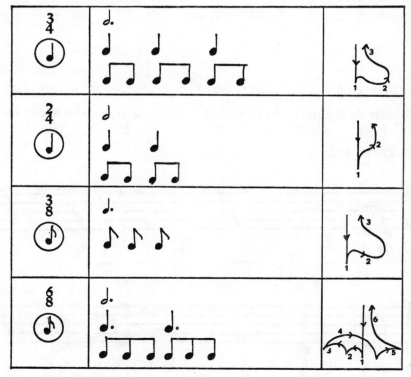

25. *Beat the Time*

* Play and sing the songs.

1.

2.

26. *Which Is Different?*

1. c	2. b	3. d	4. d
5. b	6. a	7. a	8. c

27. *A Meter Quiz*

1. 2	2. 1	3. 1/2	4. 1/8
5. 4	6. 2	7. 1	8. 1/2

"Theme from Ninth Symphony" (The last four measures are the same as the first four.)

1 1 1 1 | 1 1 1 1 | 1 1 1 1 | 1-1/2 1/2 2 |

"The Arkansas Traveler"

Section VI
EXAMINING SCALES AND KEY SIGNATURES

No.	Activity Title	Skill Involved
16.	OBEY THE ORDER	(Drawing and memorizing the order of sharps)
17.	LEARN THE LINE-UP	(Drawing and memorizing the order of flats)
18.	BUILD MAJOR SCALES IN SHARPS	(Writing scales using up to four sharps)
19.	BUILD MAJOR SCALES IN FLATS	(Writing scales using up to four flats)
20.	THINK THE NOTE ABOVE	(Writing ♯ key signatures and naming tonic key)
21.	FIND THE KEY IN FLATS	(Naming ♭ key signatures and drawing the keynote)
22.	DRAW THE SHARPS	(Drawing correct number of sharps)
23.	DRAW THE FLATS	(Drawing correct number of flats)
24.	"B" SHARP	(Writing scales using sharps and marking 1/2 steps)
25.	DOWN WITH FLATS	(Writing scales using flats and marking 1/2 steps)
26.	CROSSWORD PUZZLE	(Reviewing facts—crossword puzzle)
27.	COMPLETE THE SENTENCES	(Recalling facts)
28.	BUILD THE SCALE STEPPER	(Recalling facts—puzzle)
29.	QUIZ ON SCALES	(Writing key signatures and scales)
30.	MEET THE MINORS	(Examining natural minor and harmonic minor scales)
31.	DOUBLE OR NOTHING	(Remembering facts)

TEACHER'S GUIDE AND ANSWER KEY

1. ADD AN ACCIDENTAL   (VI–1)

The notes A, B, C, D, E, F and G are "Natural" notes. There are also other notes called SHARPS and FLATS, and they are found between most of the natural notes. "Sharped" notes are marked with a sharp sign, and "Flatted" notes are marked with a flat sign.

♯ is a SHARP sign. It raises the sound of a note by ½ step.

♭ is a FLAT sign. It lowers the sound of a note by ½ step.

♮ is a NATURAL sign. It cancels a sharp or flat. When written in front of a note, it tells us that a natural note is played or sung instead of a sharp or flat which was marked earlier.

Sharps, flats and natural signs that are written in when needed are called ACCIDENTALS. Accidentals affect all notes on the same line or space which follow in the measure.

When writing letter names of notes, place the Accidental after the letter name. For example, E Flat is written E♭ . When writing Accidentals on the staff, place the Sharp (♯) or Flat (♭) in front of the note (♯♩, ♭♩).

Draw the following notes on the staffs using Whole Notes. Add the correct Accidental for each. See the first example.

F♯   1. B♭   2. C̄♯   3. C̄♮   4. E♭   5. A♭   6. A♮

7. E♭   8. G♯   9. A♯   10. F̄♯   11. D♭   12. G♭   13. G♮

14. D♯   15. D̄♯   16. C♮   17. D̄♭   18. C♯   19. D♮   20. Ḡ♯

2. HOW GOOD IS YOUR AIM?

How good is your aim? Your targets are Sharps, Flats and Naturals.

a. Draw the clef signs at the beginning of each staff.
b. Circle the notes that are "flatted" on the staff.
c. Draw an "X" under the notes that are played "Sharp."
d. Underline the notes with the "Natural" sign.

3. SHARPS VS. FLATS

SHARPS AND FLATS

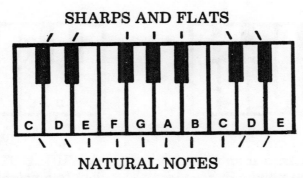

NATURAL NOTES

The keyboard shows the position of the Sharps and Flats and the Natural Notes. There are no Sharps or Flats between E and F or B and C. As you can see, there are Sharps and Flats between all other notes. The Sharp note to the right of C (between C and D) is called "C Sharp"—written C♯. The Sharp note to the right of D is D Sharp—written D♯. The other Sharp notes are F♯, G♯ and A♯.

1. On the keyboard write the names of the Natural notes and the Sharp notes. The first one of each is done for you.

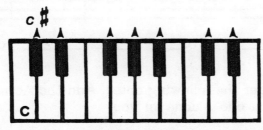

A Sharp note is played on the key that is to the right of the Natural note. A Flat note is played on the key that is to the left of the Natural note. The Flat note to the left of D (between D and C) is called "D Flat"—written D♭. The Flat note to the left of E is E Flat. The other Flat notes on the keyboard are G Flat, A Flat and B Flat.

2. On the keyboard, write the names of the Natural notes and the Flat notes. The first one of each is done for you.

From studying your keyboard you can see that some notes can be thought of as having both a Flat and a Sharp name. For example, A♯ is the same as B♭.

3. Write out the Flat names for the following Sharp notes:

C♯ = _____   D♯ = _____   F♯ = _____

4. *WATCH YOUR STEP*   (VI–4)

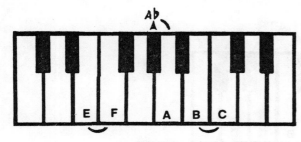

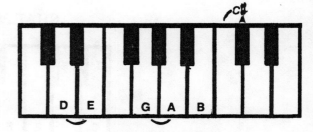

½ STEP   WHOLE STEP

A HALF STEP is the distance from one key to the nearest key with no key in between. Examples are: E to F, A♭ to A, and B to C.

A WHOLE STEP is the distance from one key to a neighbor key with one key in between. Examples are: D to E, G to A, and B to C♯.

1. Show which notes have Whole Steps and which have Half Steps between them by writing 1 for the Whole Step and ½ for the Half Step. The first example is done for you. (Refer to the keyboards above to check your answers.)

_____ ½ _____   a. _____   b. _____   c. _____   d. _____   e. _____

2. Write the letter names under the following notes. Add the Accidentals, and then mark the ½ steps with a '∨." The first one is done for you.

E♭ ∨

3. The second note in each measure is missing. The arrow (⬆ or ⬇) below the staff shows the position of the missing note. The number (1 or ½) tells the distance. Write the missing notes on the staff. The first one is done for you.

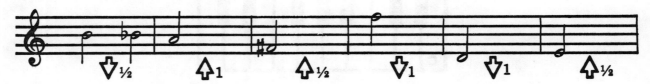

⬇½   ⬆1   ⬆½   ⬇1   ⬇1   ⬆½

5. STATE THE STEP   (VI–5)

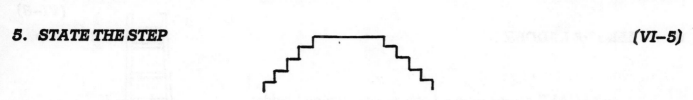

An INTERVAL is the distance between two notes. The smallest Interval studied in music is called a HALF STEP. It is the distance between two keys that are right next to each other on the keyboard.

1. Write "½" or "1" under each set of notes to indicate if the notes are a Half Step or a Whole Step apart.

a. _____   b. _____   c. _____   d. _____

e. _____   f. _____   g. _____   h. _____

i. _____   j. _____   k. _____   l. _____

2. Draw a note in each measure, up or down as the arrow shows, the distance of ½ or 1 Whole Step away from the note that you see.

a. Whole Step ⬆   b. ½ Step ⬇   c. ½ Step ⬆   d. Whole Step ⬇

6. SCALE THE LADDER

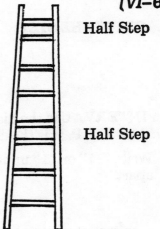

Half Step

Half Step

The word SCALE comes from a Latin word meaning "ladder." A scale consists of different tones that go up and down in pitch. Think of these tones as moving stepwise up and down a ladder.

The following is an example of a MAJOR SCALE. The Major Scale uses the seven letters of the Musical Alphabet. The tones are in alphabetical order and the scale begins and ends on the same letter. We can actually say there are eight tones in all, covering an OCTAVE.

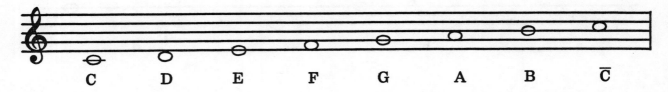

C   D   E   F   G   A   B   C̄

The tones are called SCALE DEGREES and are numbered 1, 2, 3, 4, 5, 6, 7, 8.

1   2   3 Half 4   5   6   7 Half 8
         Step   Step

The Major Scale is a series of Whole Steps and Half Steps. The Half Steps are between Scale Degrees 3 and 4, and 7 and 8. All other steps are Whole Steps.

1. Mark the Half Steps on the keyboard with this sign " ∨ ."
2. Label the Whole Steps and Half Steps on the staff by writing "1" or "½" under the " ∨ " signs. Write the note names under the notes.

C D E F G A B C̄

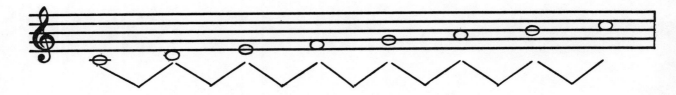

Name _____   Score _____

Date _____   Class _____

7. DRAW THE C MAJOR SCALE   (VI–7)

This is the "C" MAJOR SCALE, also known as the scale for the KEY OF "C" MAJOR. The Key gets its name from the first note of the scale, which is C. The scale starts on C and ends on C. We say that a piece is in the Key of C Major when it is based upon the notes named in this scale.

1. Write the letter name for each note on the space below the staff.
2. Between the letter names, write "1" for Whole Step or "½" for Half Step to indicate the distance between the notes.

C MAJOR SCALE

3. Draw the Whole Notes on the staff to match the letter names given below.
4. Write the name "C MAJOR SCALE" in the space above the staff.

    C   D   E   F   G   A   B   C̄

5. Draw the Treble Clef sign on the staff below.
6. On the staff write the C Major Scale using Whole Notes.
7. Under each note write its Scale Degree.
8. To show where the Half Steps are, write "½" between the proper Scale Degrees.
9. Write the name of the scale in the space above the staff.

8. NOTE THE KEYNOTE   (VI–8)

The first or starting note of a scale is called the KEYNOTE. The Keynote is also referred to as the TONIC KEY or TONAL CENTER.

1. Circle the Keynote in the scale below.

2. How many different letters does a Major Scale use? _____

3. What does the word "scale" mean? _____

4. Because a scale begins and ends on the same letter, which two numbers are interchangeable?

_____

5. What name do we call the eight tones in a scale? _____

6. A Half Step is found between Scale Degrees 3 and 4. Where is the other Half Step found? _____

7. What Degree of the Scale is the Keynote? _____

8. How many notes on the scale does an Octave cover? _____

9. a. On the staff below, draw each note of the C Major Scale. The Scale Degrees are given.
   b. Circle the pairs of notes that have a Half Step between them.
   c. Write the word KEYNOTE under the proper note.

9. WHAT'S IN A KEY?   (VI–9)

The Sharps and Flats written at the beginning of music make up what are known as KEY SIGNA-TURES. They are written on each staff after the Clef sign and show two things:

1. The notes to be raised (♯) or lowered (♭) throughout the entire song.
2. The Keynote or Tonic Key of the song.

There are on a keyboard, and there is a  to open the door.

Before a new melody is written, a Key must be decided upon. A Key indicates a particular scale or system of tones. The Key gets its name from the Keynote or the first note of the scale.

It is important that a song is pitched at a suitable level for singing. For example, "Jingle Bells" is usually written in the Key of G Major. If it were written in a lower Key, such as C Major, it would be pitched too low for some voices. Also, it is a happy song, and in a low Key it would sound more like a sad song.

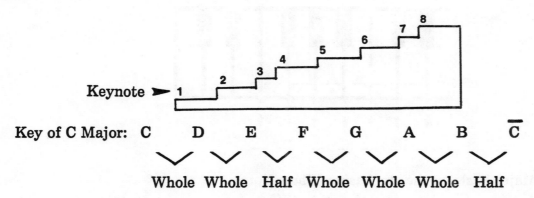

Circle all the words about SCALES and KEY SIGNATURES in the word puzzle below. Use these words to complete the sentences to the right.

M	S	H	A	R	P	O
A	E	C	L	E	F	M
J	E	T	A	N	I	F
O	T	O	M	L	V	I
R	W	O	S	E	E	R
T	O	I	X	M	T	S
I	M	O	F	L	A	T

1. The Key is based on the first degree of the _____.
2. There are _____ Half Steps in a Major Scale.
3. The Key gets its name from the _____ note of the scale.
4. There are _____ Whole Steps in a Major Scale.
5. A _____ is used to lower a tone.
6. A _____ is used to raise a tone.
7. The Key Signature is found after the _____.
8. There are no Sharps or Flats in the Key of C _____.

Name _____   Score _____

Date _____   Class _____

10. *GO BACK TO BASICS*

This is your basic scale. It can be played on the white keys of any keyboard instrument.

1. What note does the C Major Scale end on? ____
2. Finish writing the Scale Degrees for the keyboard below.

SCALE DEGREES   <u>1</u> __ __ __ __ __ __ __

3. Finish writing the letter names of the keys on the keyboard below.
4. Below the keyboard, write "1" for Whole Step or "½" for Half Step to show the distance between the Scale Degrees.

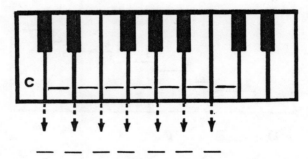

5. Write the C Major Scale on the staff using Whole Notes.
6. Write the letter names of the notes below the staff.

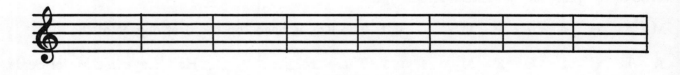

All Major Scales have the same organization of Whole Steps and Half Steps. In the C Major Scale, Sharps and Flats are not needed for this sequence to come out right.

7. On the lines below, write "1" for Whole Step and "½" for Half Step to show the distance between the Scale Degrees of a Major Scale.

SCALE DEGREES: 1   2   3   4   5   6   7   8
1 or ½ step?   ___   ___   ___   ___   ___   ___   ___

11. ANALYZE A SONG   (VI–11)

This is the Scale of C Major.

The following song is written in the Key of C (Major).

Study the above melody to answer the following:

1. On what Scale Degree does the song begin? _____
2. On what Scale Degree does the song end? _____
3. Underline the measure that has a group of notes that match the first four Scale Degrees.
4. Circle the pairs of notes that have a half tone or Half Step between them.
5. When there are no Sharps or Flats in the Key Signature, we know the song is in the Key of
   _____ (or a minor).*
6. The distance from E to F is _____ step.
7. The distance from G to A is two Half Steps or _____.
8. All Major _____ use the same pattern: Whole Step, Whole Step, Half Step, Whole Step,
   Whole Step, Whole Step, Half Step.
9. If you can name the above song, write its title here. _____

* There is another set of Keys known as the minor Keys that share the same Key Signature as the
  Major Key.

12. FROM KEYS TO KEY SIGNATURES   (VI–12)

Music is written in different keys to provide variety for both the listener and the performer. There are also other reasons. A song in one key may be too high or too low for you, but just right in another key. Sometimes music is too difficult to play in one key so it is "rearranged" in an easier key.

You can start on any tone or note and build a scale. This scale starts on "G," five Scale Degrees from C. It is the scale for the Key of G Major.

1. Finish writing the letter names of the notes for the G Major Scale.
   G MAJOR SCALE

G ___   ___   ___   ___   ___   ___   ___

2. Finish naming the keys on the keyboard
   for the G Major Scale.

3. Where are the Half Steps in this scale?

   Between ____ and ____, and ____ and
   ____.

4. Why is "F Sharp" used in this scale instead of the "Natural" F? _____

KEY SIGNATURES are Sharp and Flat signs shown on the staff right after the clef sign. A piece that is written in the Key of G Major has one Sharp in its Key Signature. The Sharp is written on the "F" line. It means that every "F" is "Sharped" unless canceled with a "Natural" sign (♮).

5. Write the Key Signature on the staff for the G Major Scale.
6. Name the notes of the scale.
7. What is the Keynote for the G Major Scale? _____
8. Under the note names write the Scale Degrees.
9. Write ½ between the Scale Degrees where the Half Steps are found.

Name _____   Score _____

Date _____   Class _____

13. "B" FLAT

This is the "F" MAJOR SCALE. The scale starts on F and ends on F. F is four Scale Degrees from C. All of the notes except B Flat are played on the white keys.

1. Finish writing the letter names of the notes for the F Major Scale.

F MAJOR SCALE

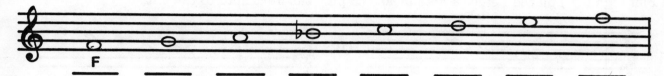

2. Finish naming the keys on the keyboard for the F Major Scale.

3. Where are the Half Steps in this scale?

   Between _____ and _____, and _____ and

   _____.

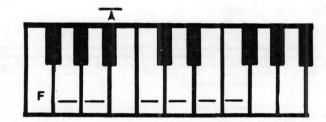

4. Why is "B Flat" used in this scale instead of the "Natural" B? _____

A song that has one Flat in its Key Signature is written in the Key of F Major. The Flat is written on the "B" line right after the clef sign. This means that every B is "Flatted" unless canceled with a "Natural" sign (♮).

5. Write the Key Signature for the F Major Scale.

6. Name the notes of the scale.

7. What is the Keynote for the F Major Scale? _____

8. Under the note names write the Scale Degrees.

9. Write ½ between the Scale Degrees where the Half Steps are found.

14. FIND THE "FLATTED" NOTES   (VI–14)

When you see one Flat (B♭)      after the Treble Clef sign, it means that all the B's throughout the piece will be "Flatted" unless preceded by a "Natural" sign. This is the "F" MAJOR Key Signature.

A Flat sign (♭) placed before a note means to play the next note to the left.

OR

1. Write the letter names under these notes. Add the Flat sign where needed.
   "Streets of Laredo"   Cowboy Song

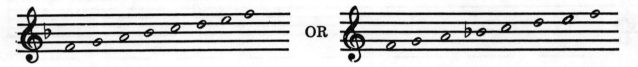

2. Circle the notes in the following song that are played on the "Flat" keys.
   "Long, Long Ago"   Thomas H. Bayly

3. Write the Key Signature for F Major on the staff below. Draw the F Major scale in Whole Notes. Circle the pairs of notes with Half Steps between them.

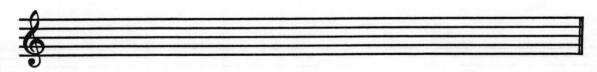

15. SCAN THE SCALES   (VI–15)

A scale gets its name from the starting note or Keynote. There are eight tones or notes in a Major Scale. This is the C Major Scale with a keyboard.

Study the SCALE CHART

SCALE CHART

The SCALE CHART shows the make-up of seven Major Scales. Notice how these scales all have the same pattern of Whole Steps and Half Steps. You can start with any note on the keyboard and play a scale. In playing a Major Scale, you will always have the same sequence of Whole Steps and Half Steps.

		1	2	3	4	5	6	7	8
Scale Degrees					½ Step			½ Step	
C	MAJOR	C	D	E	F	G	A	B	C
F	MAJOR	F	G	A	B♭	C	D	E	F
B♭	MAJOR	B♭	C	D	E♭	F	G	A	B♭
E♭	MAJOR	E♭	F	G	A♭	B♭	C	D	E♭
G	MAJOR	G	A	B	C	D	E	F♯	G
D	MAJOR	D	E	F♯	G	A	B	C♯	D
A	MAJOR	A	B	C♯	D	E	F♯	G♯	A

An ALTERED STEP is a tone either raised a Half Step by a Sharp (♯) or lowered a Half Step by a Flat (♭). An Altered Step may also be called an ALTERED TONE.

By reading across the Scale Chart, find the Altered Steps for the following scales. Write the letter names of the Altered Steps on the spaces.

1. F   Major Scale _____   4. G   Major Scale _____

2. B♭ Major Scale _____   5. D   Major Scale _____

3. E♭ Major Scale _____   6. A   Major Scale _____

Name _____   Score _____

Date _____   Class _____

16. OBEY THE ORDER   (VI–16)

The Sharps or Flats in the Key Signature are always written in the same order. In a Key Signature containing Sharps, the first Sharp is found on the "F" line, the second Sharp on the "C" space, the third Sharp on the "G" line, and so on through D, A, E and B.

To memorize the sequence F – C – G – D – A – E – B, concentrate on the placement of the first two Sharps. The rest will come easy. By memorizing this order, it will also help you to know how the Flats go on the staff. The letters F – C – G – D – A – E – B from right to left show you the order of the Flats in the Key Signature.

Memorize this order:

Write the order of the Sharps twice on the following staff. Then write the names of the Sharps on the blanks below the staff.

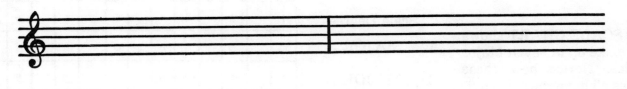

Now fold this sheet of paper on the dotted line. Read the directions.

Can you name the order in which the Sharps are always written on the staff?

1. _____   2. _____   3. _____   4. _____   5. _____   6. _____   7. _____

Can you draw the order of Sharps on the staff below?

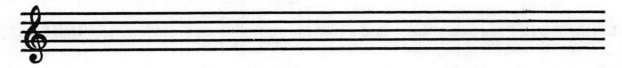

Now unfold your paper and check your answers. If you have all the answers correct, you have done a good job of memorizing the order, so color the star.

Name _____   Score _____

Date _____   Class _____

17. *LEARN THE LINE-UP*   (VI–17)

The Flats and Sharps in the Key Signature are always written in the same order. In a Key Signature containing Flats, the first Flat is found on the "B" line, the second Flat in the "E" space, the third Flat in the "A" space, and so on through D, G, C and F. Memorize this order: B – E – A – D – G – C – F.

Write the order of the Flats twice on the following staff. Then write the name of the Flats below the staff.

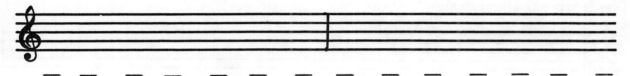

Write the Key Signature for each of the following:

1. One Flat

2. Two Flats

3. Three Flats

4. Four Flats

5. Five Flats

6. Six Flats

7. Seven Flats

18. BUILD MAJOR SCALES IN SHARPS

C MAJOR SCALE

The C Major Scale is the basic pattern for ALL Major scales.

To build the scale with one Sharp, go up FIVE Scale Degrees from C. That gives you G, the Keynote for the G Major Scale. Always go up five Scale Degrees from the previous Keynote to find the next "Sharp" scale. Five Scale Degrees from G is D, so your next scale is D Major. Continue in this way to build the A Major and E Major Scales.

Write the following scales. Write in the Key Signatures or place Sharps before the "Sharped" notes.

1. One Sharp – G Major Scale

2. Two Sharps – D Major Scale

3. Three Sharps – A Major Scale

4. Four Sharps – E Major Scale

19. BUILD MAJOR SCALES IN FLATS   (VI–19)

C MAJOR SCALE

The C Major Scale is the basic pattern for ALL Major scales.

To build a scale with one Flat, go up FOUR Scale Degrees from C. That gives you F, the Keynote for the F Major Scale. To find the next "Flat" scale, always go up four Scale Degrees from the previous Keynote. Four Scale Degrees from F is B♭, so your next scale is B♭ Major. Continue in this way to build the E♭ Major and A♭ Major Scales.

Write the following scales. Write in the Key Signatures or place Flats before the "Flatted" notes.

1. One Flat – F Major Scale

2. Two Flats – B♭ Major Scale

3. Three Flats – E♭ Major Scale

4. Four Flats – A♭ Major Scale

20. THINK THE NOTE ABOVE   (VI–20)

You may find it helpful to play or sing the Scale of the Key of a piece of music before starting to read it. It may help you get the feeling of the Key and to know which notes to expect.

To find the Key of a piece using Sharps in the Key Signature, do two things:

a. Find the last Sharp to the right.

b. Find the Tonic Key or Keynote by naming the letter in the Musical Alphabet that is ½ step up from the last Sharp. (Think one note above the last Sharp.)

Examples:

Key of G—one note above
the last Sharp

Key of D—one note above
the last Sharp

For each of the following, write the name of the Major Key Signature. After each Key Signature draw a Whole Note in the proper place on the staff to show the Tonic Key.

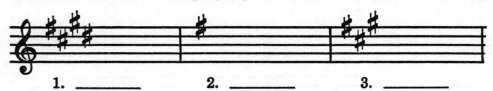

1. _____   2. _____   3. _____

4. _____   5. _____

6. _____

21. FIND THE KEY IN FLATS   (VI–21)

To find the Key of a piece of music using Flats in the Key Signature, think "next-to-the-last-Flat." Study the examples. Music that is written with three Flats is in the Key of E Flat. If the Key Signature shows four Flats, the music is in the Key of A Flat. An exception is the Key of F with one Flat.

Examples: **Exception**

Key of E Flat   Key of A Flat   Key of F (only one Flat)

Draw the Keynote in each measure. Then write the names of the Keys below the staff. The first one is done for you.

A♭   1._____   2._____   3._____   4._____   5._____

Draw the correct number of Flats on the staff to match the Keys. Place the Flats in the correct order and position. (The "fat" part of the Flat is drawn through the line or space that is to be "Flatted.")

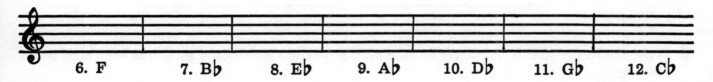

6. F   7. B♭   8. E♭   9. A♭   10. D♭   11. G♭   12. C♭

Name _____   Score _____

Date _____   Class _____

22. DRAW THE SHARPS   (VI—22)

a. Draw the Treble Clef sign at the beginning of each staff.
b. Draw the proper Key Signature on each staff after the Treble Clef.
c. Draw the Tonic note on each staff. Use Whole Notes.

1. Key of C Major

2. Key of E Major

3. Key of D Major

4. Key of G Major

5. Key of B Major

6. Key of A Major

d. Write the Key Signature correctly on each staff after the Treble Clef sign. Under each staff name the Key.

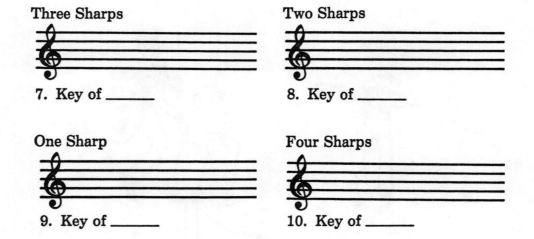

Three Sharps

7. Key of _____

Two Sharps

8. Key of _____

One Sharp

9. Key of _____

Four Sharps

10. Key of _____

23. DRAW THE FLATS (VI–23)

a. Draw the Treble Clef sign at the beginning of each staff.
b. Write the proper Key Signature on each staff after the Treble Clef sign.
c. Draw the Tonic note on each staff. Use Whole Notes.

1. Key of C Major

2. Key of A♭ Major

3. Key of B♭ Major

4. Key of D♭ Major

5. Key of F Major

6. Key of E♭ Major

d. Write the Key Signature correctly on each staff after the Treble Clef sign.
e. Name the Key under each staff.

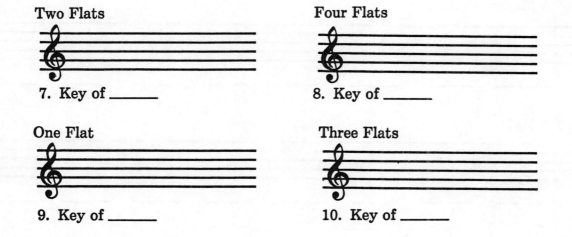

Two Flats

7. Key of _____

Four Flats

8. Key of _____

One Flat

9. Key of _____

Three Flats

10. Key of _____

Name _____   Score _____

Date _____   Class _____

24. "B" SHARP

a. Write the proper Key Signature on each staff after the Treble Clef sign.
b. Complete writing the scale for each Key. The C Major Scale is given.
c. Mark the Half Steps with a "⋀" between the pairs of Whole Notes.
d. Write the names of the notes for each scale.

1. Key of C Major

2. Key of G Major

3. Key of D Major

4. Key of A Major

5. Key of E Major

25. DOWN WITH FLATS   (VI–25)

a. Write the proper Key Signature on each staff after the Treble Clef sign.
b. Complete writing the scale for each Key. The C Major Scale is given.
c. Mark the Half Steps with a " $\vee$ " between the pairs of Whole Notes.
d. Write the names of the notes for each scale.

1. Key of C Major

2. Key of F Major

3. Key of B♭ Major

4. Key of E♭ Major

5. Key of A♭ Major

26. CROSSWORD PUZZLE   (VI-26)

Across

1. Extra Sharp ( ), Flat (♭) or Natural (♮) signs that are not included in the Key Signature are placed in _____ of the notes on the staff.

2. Sharps (♯) _____ the pitch of a note.

3. An Accidental sign is placed behind the _____ name (F ♯).

Down

4. Naturals (♮) _____ the effect of a Sharp or Flat.

5. Flats (♭) _____ the pitch of a note.

6. Sharps or Flats may be placed in front of _____ to raise or lower their pitch.

27. COMPLETE THE SENTENCES   (VI–27)

Complete the sentences below by writing in the missing letters or numbers.

1. A series of notes arranged in step is called a S __ __ __ __.

2. Pitches organized into a melody are based on a K __ __.

3. You use only the white keys on a keyboard when you play the __ Major Scale.

4. Scales are written on the S__ __ __ __.

5. The following letters give you the order of the Sharps on the staff: F __ __ __ __ __ __.

6. A Sharp raises the sound of a tone by __ step.

7. The distance from one key to another with no key in between is __ step.

8. The distance from one key to another key is called an I __ __ __ __ __ __ __.

9. The word "scale" comes from the Latin word meaning L __ __ __ __ __.

10. The Major Scale uses the letters of the Musical A __ __ __ __ __ __ __.

11. The first note in a scale is called the K __ __ __ __ __ __.

12. The Keynote may be referred to as the Tonal Center or T __ __ __ __.

13. Sharps and Flats are always written in a set O __ __ __ __.

14. The following letters give you the order of the Flats on the staff: B __ __ __ __ __ __.

15. A Sharp or Flat is canceled out by a N __ __ __ __ __ sign.

16. The numbered tones of a scale are called S __ __ __ __   D __ __ __ __ __ __.

17. There are __ tones in a Major Scale.

18. The Half Steps in a Major Scale are between Scale Degrees __ and __, and __ and __.

19. The Key Signature is placed after the C __ __ __ sign.

20. The Key of D Major has __ Sharps.

28. BUILD THE SCALE STEPPER   *(VI–28)*

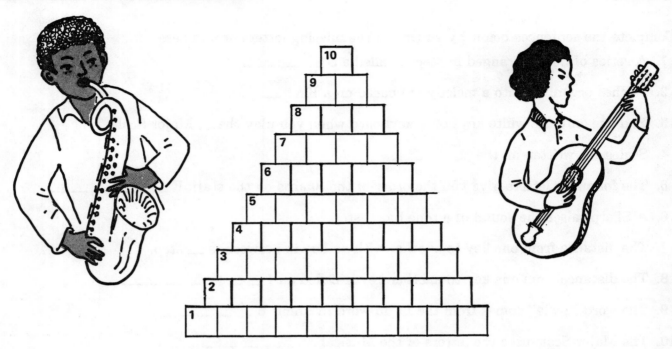

Write the missing answers in the above boxes for the SCALE STEPPER. Start at the bottom and build up.

1. A sign written before a note to indicate a chromatic alteration is called an
   __ __ __ __ __ __ __ __ __ __.
2. The Sharps or Flats at the beginning of a piece that indicate the Key the music is written in is the Key __ __ __ __ __ __ __ __ __.
3. The order of Half Steps and Whole Steps on which a Major Scale is based upon is called a
   __ __ __ __ __ __ __ __ __.
4. Music is said to be in a particular Key when it is based upon the scale starting with the
   __ __ __ __ __ __ __ of the same name.
5. The F Major Scale starts on the __ __ __ __ __ __ Scale Degree from C.
6. A series of tones going up or down in pitch according to a certain scheme is called a __ __ __ __ __.
7. In the F Major Scale, the distance between G and A is a Whole __ __ __ __.
8. The Sharps and Flats in the Key Signature tell you what __ __ __ the song is in.
9. Name the missing tone: __ __ re mi fa sol la ti do.
10. When a song has no Sharps or Flats, it makes use of the tones that belong to the a Minor or __ Major Scale.

Name _____   Score _____

Date _____   Class _____

29. QUIZ ON SCALES

Write the names of the Key Signatures. Write the scale on each staff with Whole Notes, and then circle the pairs of notes with Half Steps between them.

1. Key of _____

2. Key of _____

3. Key of _____

4. Key of _____

5. Key of _____

6. Key of _____

7. Key of _____

30. *MEET THE MINORS*

A MINOR SCALE originates from its RELATIVE MAJOR SCALE. It is called "Relative" because both scales have the same Key Signature. The minor scale is built on the sixth step of the Major Scale. This form of minor is called the "Natural Minor Scale" or "Pure Minor Mode."

Example: G Major Scale   Natural Minor Scale

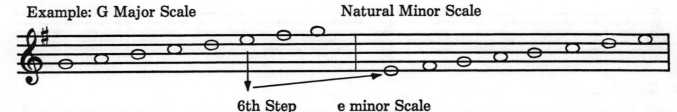

6th Step   e minor Scale

1. Write the Natural Minor Scale for the C Major Scale on the staff lines below.

C Major Scale   Natural Minor Scale

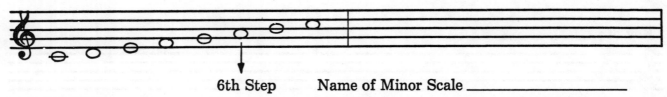

6th Step   Name of Minor Scale _____

The HARMONIC Minor Scale is the most commonly used of the minor scales. This scale uses the same notes as the Natural Minor Scale except for the seventh step of the scale. An accidental is always used to raise the seventh degree of the scale by ½ step.

Example: e minor scale (Harmonic Minor Scale)

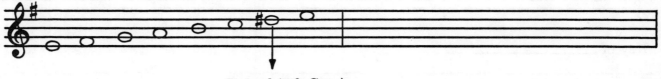

Raised (7th Step)

2. Write the A harmonic minor scale on the staff below.

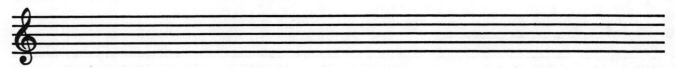

Here are some clues for finding out if a piece is written in a minor key.

1. Look at the first and last notes of a piece for minor scale notes.

2. Listen for a minor sound.

3. Count up six degrees from the Major Keynote, or count down three Half Steps from the Major Key.

4. Find the name of the Relative minor Key if the piece ends two alphabet letters lower than the Major Key.

Name _____   Score _____

Date _____   Class _____

31. DOUBLE OR NOTHING   (VI–31)

Can you answer this twin quiz?

1. Name TWO notes with stems. _____

2. Name TWO dotted notes. _____

3. Name TWO Key Signatures with Flats. _____

4. Name TWO Key Signatures with Sharps. _____

5. Name TWO kinds of Rests. _____

6. Name TWO Clefs. _____

7. Name TWO letters of the Musical Alphabet. _____

8. Name TWO notes that are not filled in. _____

9. Name TWO places where Leger Lines may be written. _____

10. Name TWO things the Time Signature tells us. _____

11. Name TWO "Natural" notes. _____

12. Name TWO "Accidental" signs. _____

13. Name TWO Major Scales. _____

14. Name TWO kinds of signs that are found in Key Signatures. _____

15. Name TWO notes that are shorter than the Half Note. _____

TEACHER'S GUIDE
AND ANSWER KEY

1. Add an Accidental
(For reference)

C Major

(C Major)

(Keynote) C

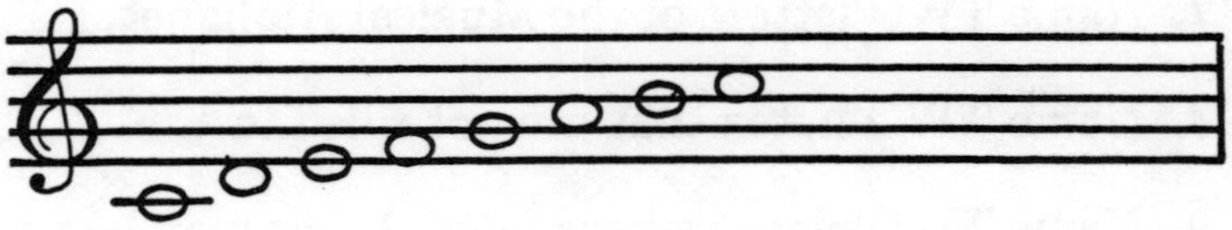

G Major

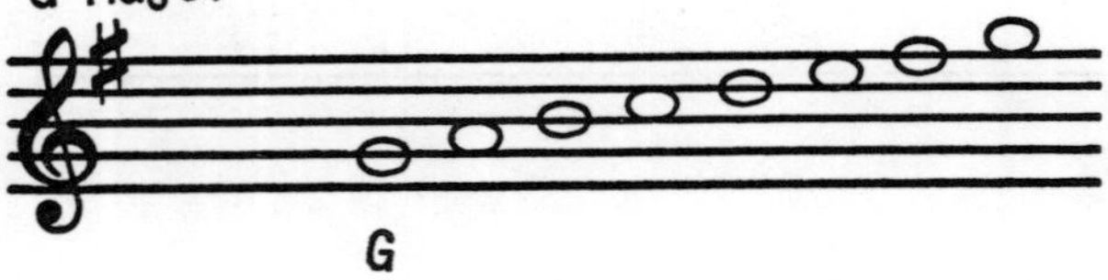

G

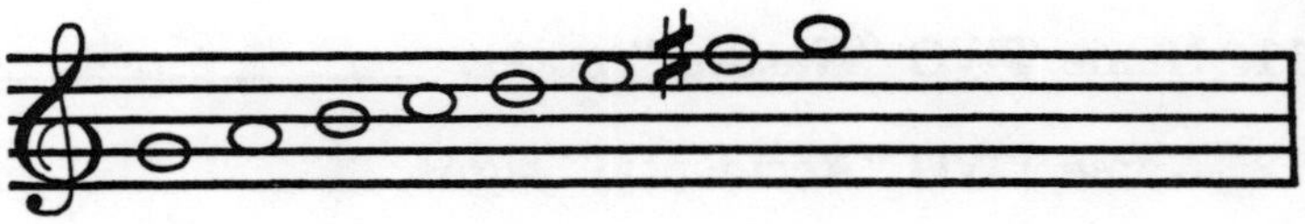

D Major

D

A Major

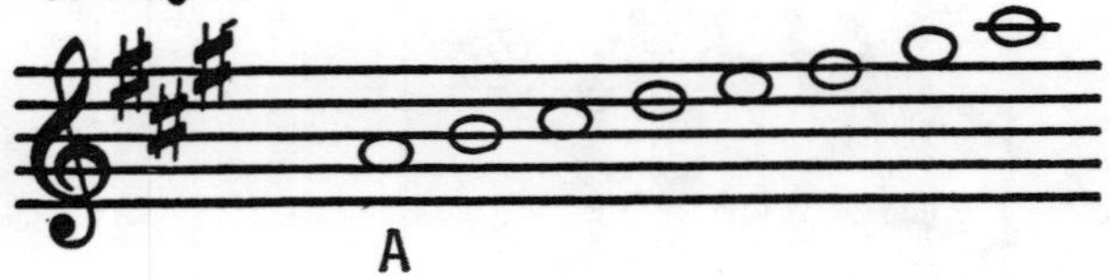

A

E Major

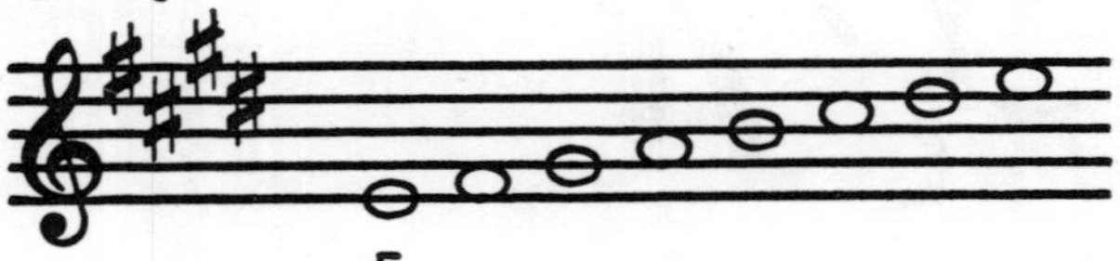

E

151

* Practice drawing Sharps, Flats and Natural signs on the chalkboard.

1. Add an Accidental

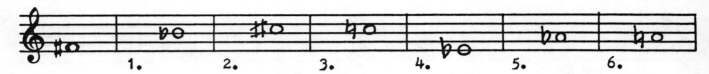

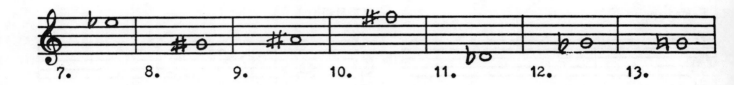

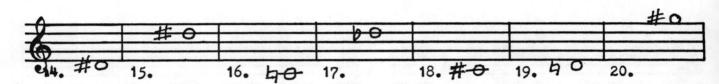

2. How Good Is Your Aim?

a. Check for proper position of Clef signs. (When directions call for Clef signs, students should draw the Treble Clef.)

b. "Flatted" notes: 1, 13, 16, 22

c. "Sharped" notes: 5, 6, 7, 10, 20

d. "Natural" notes: 3, 11, 14, 21

3. Sharps Vs. Flats

Practice finding Sharps, Flats, and the Natural notes on the keyboard.

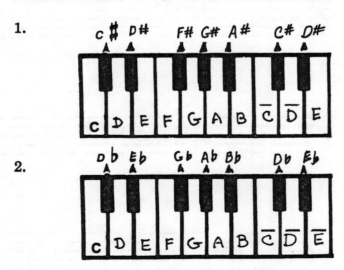

3. D Flat, E Flat, G Flat

4. *Watch Your Step*

1. a. ½   b. ½   c. 1   d. 1   e. ½

2.

3.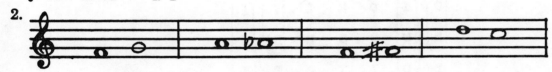

* The examples show Whole Steps and Half Steps going up the keyboard. Practice finding Whole Steps and Half Steps going in the reverse direction, down the keyboard.

5. *State the Step*

1. a. ½   b. 1   c. ½   d. 1   e. ½   f. 1   g. 1   h. 1   i. 1
   j. ½   k. ½   l. 1

2.

Students should have access to the keyboard while doing this exercise.

6. *Scale the Ladder*

1. Mark only the ½ steps that occur between the white keys on the keyboard. The "V" marks will be between E and F, and B and C̄.
2. The note names and numbers appear in the following order:
   C   1   D   1   E   ½   F   1   G   1   A   1   B   ½   C

7. *Draw the C Major Scale*

1. See activity 6.
2. See activity 6.
3. See the scale on the page.
4. - - - - - -
5-6. See scale on the page.
7. 1 – 2 – 3 – 4 – 5 – 6 – 7 – 8
8. Write ½ between 3 and 4, and between 7 and 8.
9. C Major Scale

8. *Note the Keynote*

1. Circle the first note "C."
2. 7
3. Ladder; a sequence of tones.

4. 1 and 8

5. Octave

6. Between 7 and 8

7. 1

8. 8

9. a. Check with scale on the page.
   b. Circle 3–4 and 7–8.
   c. Write "Keynote" under the first note "C" above "1."

9. *What's in a Key?*

1. scale   2. two   3. first   4. five   5. flat   6. sharp   7. clef   8. Major

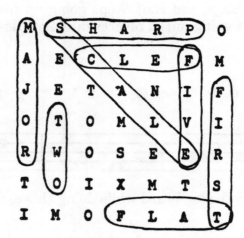

* Students can find songs with different Key Signatures and tell which notes would be "Flatted" or "Sharped."

* If someone plays an instrument, he or she could demonstrate how a song sounds higher or lower in a different key.

10. *Go Back to Basics*

1. $\overline{C}$

2. 2 – 3 – 4 – 5 – 6 – 7 – 8

3. Check with keyboard on the page.

4. 1 1 ½ 1 1 1 ½

5. Check scale in activity 7.

6. See activity 7.

7. Same as 4 above.

Students should be given the opportunity to practice playing the C Major Scale both up and down the keyboard. The question should be asked: Why is the C Major Scale considered to be our basic scale? Answer: All other Major Scales are built on the same sequence of Whole Steps and Half Steps that you find in the C Major Scale.

11. Analyze a Song

1. 5   2. 1   3. Top staff, third measure

4.

5. C   6. ½   7. 1 step   8. Scales   9. "Lightly Row." Students should be given the opportunity to play the piece. The song could also be sung according to the diatonic scale: sol mi mi, fa re re, do re mi fa, sol sol sol, etc.

* For ear training, students should be able to write on the staff the sequence from the fifth to the third as it is played on the keyboard. They will begin to associate this sequence with the beginning bar of "Lightly Row." Introduce the word "bar," another name for "measure."
* Review SLUR (a curved line connecting notes of different pitch).

12. From Keys to Key Signatures

1. A, B, C̄, D̄, Ē, F Sharp, Ḡ
2. A, B, C̄, D̄, Ē, F Sharp (written over black key with arrow), Ḡ
3. B – C̄ and F̄ Sharp – Ḡ
4. F Sharp has to be "Sharped" for the sequence to come out right.
5. The Sharp is written on the top line (F) to the right of the Clef.
6. G, A, B, C̄, D̄, Ē, F Sharp, Ḡ
7. G – the note on which the scale begins
8. Scale Degrees: 1, 2, 3, 4, 5, 6, 7, 8.
9. ½ is written between 3–4, and 7–8.

* Students should be given the opportunity to play the G Major Scale and to sing songs written in this Key.

13. "B" Flat

1. G, A, B Flat, C̄, D̄, Ē, F̄
2. G, A, B Flat (written over the black key with arrow), C̄, D̄, Ē, F̄
3. A – B Flat, and Ē – F̄
4. B Flat has to be used for the sequence to come out right.
5. The Key Signature (one Flat) is written after the Clef on the middle line (B).
6. F, G, A, B Flat, C̄, D̄, Ē, F̄
7. F

8. 1 – 2 – 3 – 4 – 5 – 6 – 7 – 8

9. ½ is written between 3–4 and 7–8.

* Students should be given the opportunity to play the F Major Scale and to sing songs written in this Key.

14. *Find the "Flatted" Notes*

1. $\overline{C}$, $\overline{C}$, B Flat, A, B Flat, $\overline{C}$, B Flat, A, G, F, E, C

2. Circle last note in first measure, second note in 3rd measure, first note in last measure

3.

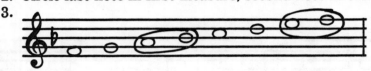

15. *Scan the Scales*

1. B (Flat)　　2. B (Flat), E (Flat)　　3. E (Flat), A (Flat), B (Flat)

4. F (Sharp)　　5. F (Sharp), C (Sharp)　　6. C (Sharp), F (Sharp), G (Sharp)

* Students should have the opportunity to play the different scales and, in doing so, note which altered step(s) are a part of each scale.

16. *Obey the Order*

1–7. Self check.

Students can test their memory by writing Key Signatures in Sharps, beginning with one Sharp.

It is important to know at a glance which notes are played "Flat" or "Sharp" in case someone takes up lessons on an instrument.

The Keys of F Sharp and C Sharp are very seldom used.

17. *Learn the Line-up*

1–7. Self check by using the line-up at the top of the page.

Students can test their memory by writing Key Signatures in Flats, beginning with one Flat.

Practice writing Key Signatures in Flats.

The Key of C Flat Major is not used because notes that sound the same are in the simpler Key of B Major.

18. *Build Major Scales in Sharps*

After the work on this page has been finished, the following question pertaining to each Key Signature could be asked: "In Music with this Key Signature, what notes would we expect?" Example: In music with one Sharp, we would expect these notes: G – A – B – C – D – E – F Sharp – G (the scale of G Major).

Sometimes you may come across the notes E Sharp and B Sharp, and even notes that are called "Double Sharps." These are not new notes, only different names for notes you already know. E Sharp is another name for F Natural. B Sharp is the name sometimes given to C Natural. A Double Sharp further Sharps a note that is already Sharp. (✖ = Double Sharped)

For answers, refer to number 1 of Section VI Answer Key.

19. *Build Major Scales in Flats*

The following question pertaining to each Key Signature could be asked: "In music with this Key Signature, what notes would we expect?" Example: In music with one Flat we would expect these notes: F – G – A – B Flat – C – D – E – F (the Scale of F Major).

* Sometimes C Flat and F Flat and notes called "Double Flats" are used. C Flat is another name for B Natural, and F Flat is another name for E Natural. In certain Keys, these notes are renamed to keep the names of notes in the scales in alphabetical order and allow Key Signatures to be written. The same note cannot be both a Flat (or Sharp) and a Natural in a Key Signature.

* A Double Flat further Flats a note that is already Flat. (♭♭ = Double Flat)

For answers to questions 1–4, refer to Number 1 of Section VI Answer Key.

20. *Think the Note Above*

1. E   2. G   3. A   4. B   5. D   6. C

For proper placement of notes refer to Number 1 of Section VI Answer Key.

21. *Find the Key in Flats*

For answers, refer to Number 1 of Section VI Answer Key.

22. *Draw the Sharps*

For answers, refer to Number 1 of Section VI Answer Key.

23. *Draw the Flats*

For answers, refer to Number 1 of Section VI Answer Key.

24. *"B" Sharp*

For answers, refer to Number 1 of Section VI Answer Key.

25. *Down With Flats*

For answers, refer to Number 1 of Section VI Answer Key.

26. *Crossword Puzzle*

1. front
2. raise
3. letter
4. cancel
5. lower
6. notes

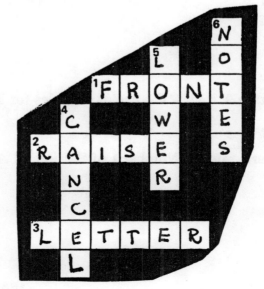

27. Complete the Sentences

1. Scale
2. Key
3. C
4. Staff
5. F – C – G – D – A – E – B
6. ½
7. ½
8. Interval
9. Ladder
10. Alphabet
11. Keynote
12. Tonic
13. Order
14. B – E – A – D – G – C – F
15. Natural
16. Scale Degrees
17. 8
18. 3–4, 7–8
19. Clef
20. 2

28. Build the Scale Stepper

1. ACCIDENTAL
2. SIGNATURE
3. SEQUENCE
4. KEYNOTE
5. FOURTH
6. SCALE
7. STEP
8. KEY
9. DO
10. C

For question 9, review the use of syllables for scale degrees.

29. Quiz on Scales

For answers, refer to Number 1 of Section VI Answer Key.

30. *Meet the Minors*

A minor Scale

1. A minor Scale

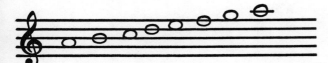

2. A Harmonic minor Scale

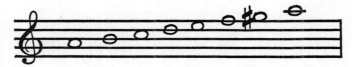

Play minor music and discuss how it sounds and when it is used (sad occasions, to frighten at Halloween, etc.). The minor can be contrasted with the major in sound.

31. *Double or Nothing*

Answers will vary.

Section VII
IDENTIFYING INTERVALS

TEACHER'S GUIDE AND ANSWER KEY

Name _____   Score _____

Date _____   Class _____

1. WRITE THE LETTER   (VII–1)

An INTERVAL is the distance from one note to another. You move by STEPS when playing up or down the keyboard on neighbor keys. Neighbor white keys are called intervals of a 2nd. An Interval is counted by the number of staff degrees covered.

1. Write the letter names of the keys moving up by intervals of a 2nd.

2. Write the letter names of the white keys moving down by intervals of a 2nd.

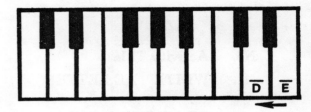

Skipped white keys are called intervals of a 3rd. For example, C to E is a 3rd and covers 3 scale degrees: C – D – E.

3. Write the letter names of the white keys moving up by intervals of a 3rd.

4. Write the letter names of the white keys moving down by intervals of a 3rd.

5. Write the letter names of the keys in the spaces to show the intervals.

   a. A 2nd (step) above   C ____   E̅ ____   B ____   A ____   D ____
   b. A 2nd (step) below   F ____   E ____   C̅ ____   G ____   A ____
   c. A 3rd (skip) above   A ____   B ____   F ____   C ____   E ____
   d. A 3rd (skip) below   G ____   D̅ ____   F ____   C̅ ____   E ____

Name _____   Score _____

Date _____   Class _____

2. DRAW THE NOTE   (VII-2)

| Interval of a 2nd (Move stepwise up or down.) | Interval of a 3rd (Skip a step up or down.) | Repeated note (Repeat the same note.) |

Use the examples above to answer the following questions.

1. From a line note to the next space note or a space note to the next line note is called a step. It is also called an interval of a _____.

2. From a line note to the next line note or a space note to the next space note is called a _____, or an interval of a 3rd.

3. Repeated notes are found either on the _____ line or space.

4. The distance between any two notes is called an _____.

For each example below, draw the second note and write its letter name on the blank. The letter name of the first note is given with the interval you are to complete.

1.	2.	3.	4.	5.
F _____	E̅ _____	A _____	B _____	C _____
up a 2nd	down a 3rd	up a 3rd	repeat	up a 2nd

6.	7.	8.	9.	10.
D _____	F _____	C̅ _____	A _____	G _____
down a 2nd	up a 3rd	down a 3rd	up a 2nd	repeat

3. THINK UP, DOWN, OR SAME   (VII–3)

1. Draw a note a step above each of the following notes.

2. Draw a note a step below each of the following notes.

3. Draw a note a skip above each of the following notes.

4. Draw a note a skip below each of the following notes.

5. Draw repeated notes.

4. WHICH: MELODIC OR HARMONIC?   (VII–4)

An INTERVAL is the distance between two notes.

The MELODIC INTERVAL is an interval of two notes sounded one after the other.

The HARMONIC INTERVAL is an interval of two notes sounded together.

Intervals may be played separately or together.

MELODIC INTERVAL

HARMONIC INTERVAL

An Interval may start on any line or space. For the examples below, circle the word Harmonic if the notes are played together. If the notes are played separately, circle the word Melodic.

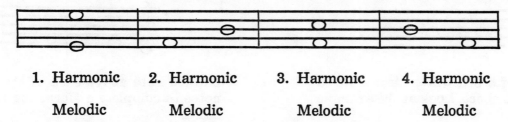

1. Harmonic   2. Harmonic   3. Harmonic   4. Harmonic

   Melodic   Melodic   Melodic   Melodic

The first note of each Interval is given below. Add the second note to complete the correct interval. The second note may be drawn any place on the staff as long as it obeys the rule for Harmonic and Melodic Intervals.

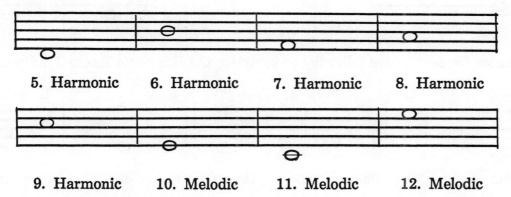

5. Harmonic   6. Harmonic   7. Harmonic   8. Harmonic

9. Harmonic   10. Melodic   11. Melodic   12. Melodic

5. USE THE NUMBERS   (VII–5)

Intervals are named for the number of lines and spaces from the bottom note through the top note.

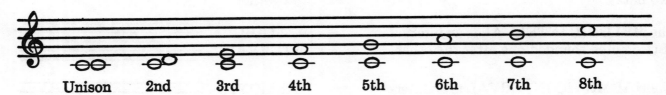

Unison   2nd   3rd   4th   5th   6th   7th   8th

An Interval of a 2nd goes from line to space or space to line. Look at the example below.

Draw a note above each of the following notes to complete a Harmonic Interval of a 2nd.

1.

An Interval of a 3rd will go from line to line or space to space. Look at the example below.

Draw a note above each of the following notes to complete a Harmonic Interval of a 3rd.

2.

Draw the top note for each of the following to complete the Harmonic Interval indicated.

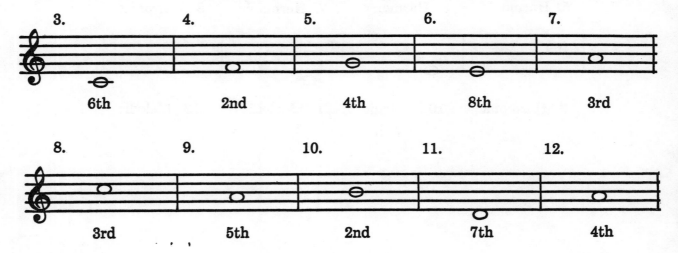

3.   4.   5.   6.   7.

6th   2nd   4th   8th   3rd

8.   9.   10.   11.   12.

3rd   5th   2nd   7th   4th

6. STEP, SKIP, OR REPEAT   (VII-6)

An INTERVAL is the distance between two notes. The second note may move stepwise, up or down, it may skip steps, or it may repeat itself.

To measure the distance of a step, count from one neighbor note to the next.

To measure the distance of a skip, count the number of lines and spaces from the bottom note through the top note.

A repeated note simply stays on the same pitch by repeating itself.

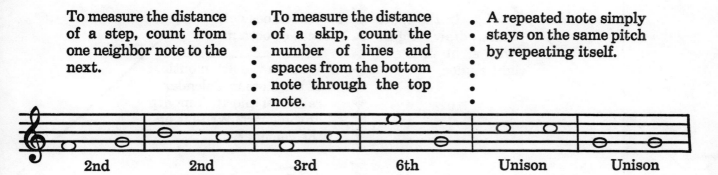

Write the names of these intervals below the staffs.

1._____   2._____   3._____   4._____

5._____   6._____   7._____   8._____

9._____   10._____   11._____   12._____

7. UNLOCK THE "OCT"   (VII–7)

By knowing the meaning of "oct," you can "unlock" the meaning of words that begin with this syllable.

1. In the space below, draw a figure with eight sides and eight angles.

2. We call this figure an octa_____.

3. What does oct, octa or octo mean?
_____

4. What is the 8th month of the Roman Calendar called (or the 10th month of the year)? Write it on the calendar.

1	2	3	4	5	6	7
8	9	10	11	12	13	14
15	16	17	18	19	20	21
22	23	24	25	26	27	28
29	30	31				

6. Draw an octopus in the water below.
7. How many legs should the octopus have?
_____

Octave Octave Octave

5. What is the 8th tone above or below a given note called?
_____
An interval of an 8th is called by the same name.

8. OVERLOOKING OCTAVES

For each of the following notes, draw another note to complete the melodic interval of an octave. The arrow shows the direction the note should be drawn.

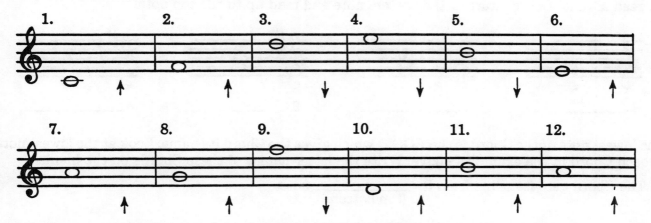

Write the letter names of the notes below the staff. Circle the octaves.

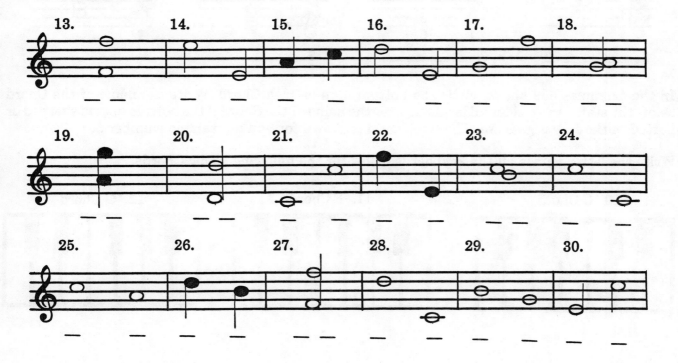

Name _____   Score _____

Date _____   Class _____

9. *THINK SNOWMAN*   *(VII—9)*

A CHORD is a group of three or more notes played at the same time. All Chords are built on different scale degrees. A Chord built on the first degree of the scale is called the I CHORD or TONIC CHORD. To read a Tonic Chord, start at the bottom note and read up to the top note.

1._____   2._____   3._____   4._____

The lowest note of the Chord is the ROOT, which gives the Chord its name. Look at the lowest note of each Chord in the examples above. Write the letter names of these Chords on the blanks.

5. The Chord gets its name from its _____ note.
                                     (top/bottom)

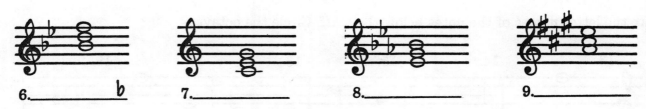

6._____ ♭   7._____   8._____   9._____

In the examples 6-9 above, circle the bottom note of each Chord. Write the name of the Chord below the staff. An Accidental is added after the name of the Chord if the bottom note is sharped or flatted in the Key Signature. The Accidental is drawn for you in example Number 6.

Write the letter names on the keyboards below for the following Tonic Chords.

10. C Chord   11. F Chord   12. G Chord

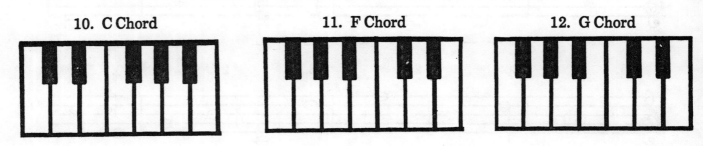

10. CREATING CHORDS   (VII–10)

There are three important chords, called PRIMARY CHORDS, used for all Major Scales. They are the chords most often used. PRIMARY CHORDS are built on the first, fourth and fifth degrees of the scale. Each of these chords has a name.

First Degree	=	I Chord	=	tonic chord
Fourth Degree	=	IV Chord	=	subdominant chord
Fifth Degree	=	V_7 Chord	=	dominant seventh chord

The V_7 Chord may be pronounced the "V (letter V) Seventh" Chord.

Roman numerals are used to tell the degrees of the scale on which the chord is built.

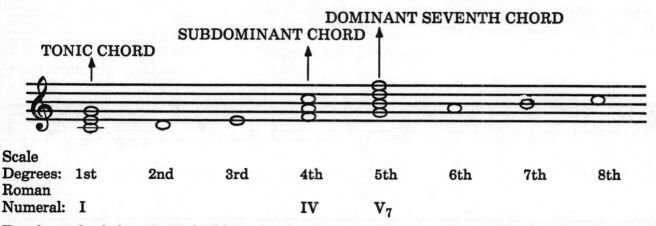

Scale Degrees:	1st	2nd	3rd	4th	5th	6th	7th	8th
Roman Numeral:	I			IV	V_7			

For the scales below, finish building the chords on the first, fourth and fifth degrees of each scale. Write the Roman numerals under the chords.

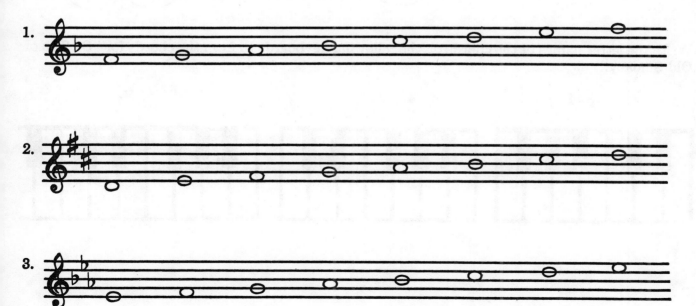

11. FIND THE COMBINATION   (VII–11)

When CHORD SYMBOLS are shown above a melody line, the pianist improvises or makes up the bass part. The CHORD SYMBOLS are used to show which chords are played for the accompaniment. These are played with the left hand.

Here's how to read the Chord Symbols:

Key of C Major	Key of G Major
I = C Chord	I = G Chord
IV = F Chord	IV = C Chord
V_7 = G_7 Chord	V_7 = D_7 Chord

1. What chords are used in the song "On Top of Old Smokey"? _____
2. In what key is the song written? _____

"On Top of Old Smokey"

Southern Mountain Song

Write the letter names of the chords on the following keyboards to form the chords for "On Top of Old Smokey."

3. I   4. IV   5. V_7

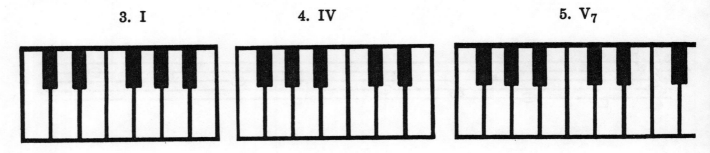

12. PLAY BINGO   (VII–12)

1. What chords are used in the song "Bingo?" _____
2. In what key is this song written? _____

"Bingo"

Write the letter names of the chords on the following keyboards to form the chords for "Bingo."

3. I   4. IV   5. V₇

TEACHER'S GUIDE
AND ANSWER KEY

1. Write the Letter

Intervals in this lesson refer to the Key of C Major which uses no sharps or flats. The scale is played on all the white keys. (Staff degrees and scale degrees are the same.)

1. E F G A B C D E   2. C D E F G A B C
3. G B D   4. D F A (from left to right)
5. a. D F C̄ B E
   b. Ē D̄ B F G
   c. C̄ D̄ A E G
   d. E B D A C

2. Draw the Note

1. second   2. skip   3. same   4. interval

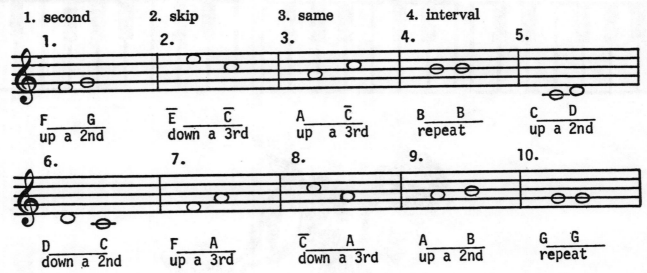

1. F _ G   2. Ē _ C̄   3. A _ C̄   4. B _ B   5. C _ D
    up a 2nd   down a 3rd   up a 3rd   repeat   up a 2nd

6. D _ C   7. F _ A   8. C̄ _ A   9. A _ B   10. G _ G
    down a 2nd   up a 3rd   down a 3rd   up a 2nd   repeat

3. Think Up, Down, or Same

1.

174

2.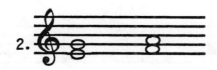

    3.–4. Answers will vary.

    5. Answers will be the same notes as shown.

4. *Which: Melodic or Harmonic?*

    1. Harmonic   2. Melodic   3. Harmonic   4. Melodic

    5.–12. Answers will vary.

5. *Use the Numbers*

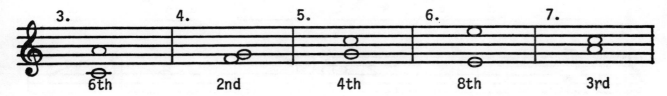

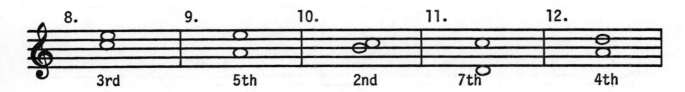

6. *Step, Skip, or Repeat*

1. Unison	2. 2nd	3. 2nd	4. 3rd
5. 5th	6. 2nd	7. 3rd	8. Unison
9. Unison	10. 2nd	11. 4th	12. 2nd

7. *Unlock the "Oct"*

    1.

    2.   -gon

3. Eight

4. October

5. Octave

6. Drawings will vary.

7. Eight

8. *Overlooking Octaves*

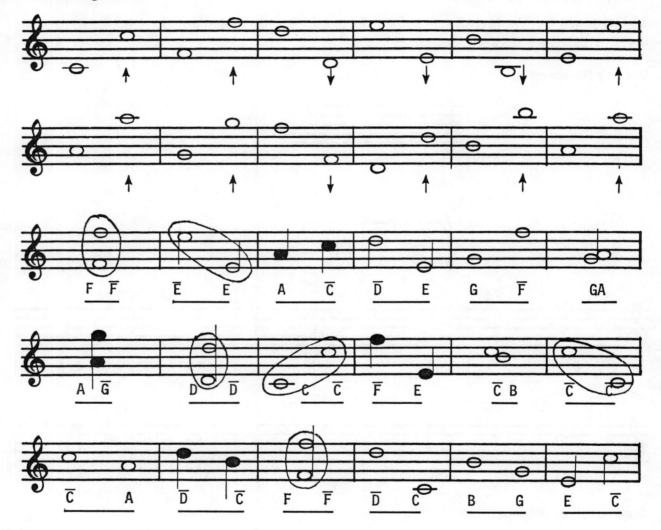

9. *Think Snowman*

1. C	2. F	3. G	4. D	5. bottom
6. B Flat	7. C	8. E Flat	9. A	(circle bottom notes in examples 6–9)

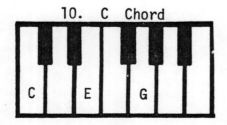
10. C Chord

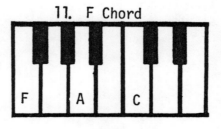
11. F Chord

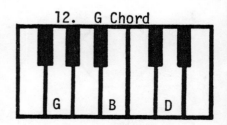
12. G Chord

10. Creating Chords

1.

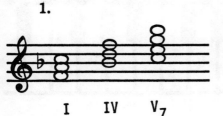

I   IV   V₇

2.

I   IV   V₇

3.

I   IV   V₇

11. Find the Combination

1. C, F and G₇
2. Key of C Major

3. I

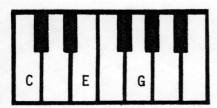

4. IV

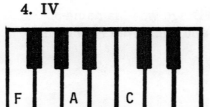

5. V₇

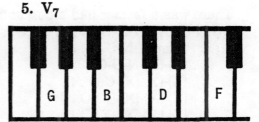

* Sing "On Top of Old Smokey" using autoharp, guitar or ukelele accompaniment. A chord should be played until a different chord is required. On this song, the accompanist would play C, F, F, F, F, C, C, C for the first line.
* Write letter names below notes.
* Review symbols: TIE, SLUR, DOTTED NOTES.

Verse 1. On top of old Smokey all covered with snow
       I lost my true lover come courtin' too slow.

2. A courtin's a pleasure, a-flirtin' brings grief,
       A false-hearted lover is worse than a thief.

3. A thief he will rob you, and take what you save,
       But a false-hearted lover will lead to your grave.

4. It's raining, it's hailing, the moon gives no light,
       My horses can't travel this dark road tonight.

5. (Repeat Verse 1.)

Tune Ukelele:

G C E A

C

G₇

F

12. Play Bingo

1. G, C and D₇
2. Key of G Major

177

3. I

G B D

4. IV

C E G

5. V$_7$

F.#

D A C

* Rewrite "Bingo" in $\frac{2}{4}$ time.
* Transpose "Bingo" to the Key of F Major. (The song will then begin on low C.) Using the Key of F Major, the following chords will be used: F, B Flat, C$_7$

"Bingo"

There was a farmer had a dog and Bingo was his name-o.
B-I-N-G-O, B-I-N-G-O, B-I-N-G-O, and Bing-o was his name-o.
2. . . . (Clap)-I-N-G-O . . .
3. . . . (X)-(X)-N-G-O . . .
4. . . . (X)-(X)-(X)-G-O . . .
5. . . . (X)-(X)-(X)-(X)-O . . .
6. . . . (X)-(X)-(X)-(X)-(X) . . .

Use autoharp, guitar or ukelele accompaniment.

Section VIII
GETTING TO KNOW SYMBOLS AND TERMS

TEACHER'S GUIDE AND ANSWER KEY

Name _____   Score _____

Date _____   Class _____

1. UNCOVER THE CLUE   (VIII-1)

See what a good detective you are by using the clues at
the left to complete the missing letters at the right.

1. It contains five lines and four spaces on which music   S _ _ _ _ _
    is written.
2. Symbols used to show pitch.   N _ _ _ _ _
3. The highness or lowness of a tone.   P _ _ _ _ _
4. Another name for the G Clef.   T _ _ _ _ _ _   C _ _ _
5. Short lines used to extend the staff.   L _ _ _ _ _   L _ _ _ _ _
6. The rate of speed at which a musical work is played   T _ _ _ _ _
    or sung.
7. The rhythm to which you count in time to music.   B _ _ _ _
8. A note with a line going through it.   L _ _ _   N _ _ _ _
9. Notes that don't have lines going through them.   S _ _ _ _ _   N _ _ _ _ _
10. What the letter names of the spaces spell.   F _ _ _
11. A filled-in note with a stem.   Q _ _ _ _ _ _ _   N _ _ _ _
12. An "open" note that has no stem.   W _ _ _ _ _   N _ _ _
13. A symbol that raises the sound of a note.   S _ _ _ _ _
14. The difference between two pitches.   I _ _ _ _ _ _ _ _ _
15. A silent beat in music.   R _ _ _ _
16. A symbol that lowers the sound of a note.   F _ _ _ _
17. A word meaning the same as "tonic."   K _ _ _ _ _ _ _
18. I, IV and V are the most important Scale _____.   D _ _ _ _ _ _ _
19. A sign that cancels Sharps and Flats.   N _ _ _ _ _ _ _
20. Another name for Time Signature.   M _ _ _ _ _

Name _____   Score _____

Date _____   Class _____

2. DRAW THE SYMBOLS   (VIII–2)

Rewrite the music on the staff after each example. Read all the definitions carefully and be sure to draw the symbols. It is not necessary to draw the Treble Clef signs.

1. The DOUBLE BAR is used to mark the end of a section of music. It divides the musical arrangement.

2. A DOUBLE BAR with the heavier second line marks the final ending of a piece of music.

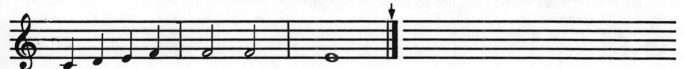

3. A REPEAT SIGN is shown by a double bar and two dots. If there is a previous Repeat Sign, return to it and repeat the section. Otherwise, return to the beginning of the music.

4. Da Capo (dah CAH-poe) means "go back to the beginning" (abbreviation: D.C.). Fine means "finish or the end." "D.C. al Fine" means "return to the beginning of the section and continue playing until Fine."

5. FIRST and SECOND ENDINGS are used when a section of music is repeated with two different endings. Both endings are marked by brackets and numbers. The First Ending is played the first time through and the Second Ending is played the second time through.

3. LABEL THE SYMBOLS   (VIII–3)

Read each definition carefully. Copy the notes and symbols on the staff lines after each example. It is not necessary to draw the Treble Clef signs.

1. A TIE is a curved line that connects two notes of the same pitch. The second note is a continuation of the first and not played separately.

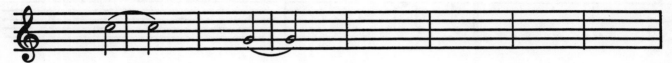

2. LEGATO (lay-GAH-toe) means "smooth, connected." A SLUR is a curved line drawn over or under two or more notes that are to be played *legato*.

3. STACCATO (stah-CAH-toe) is the opposite of *legato*. Staccato notes are disconnected, detached, crisp and separated. Staccato touch is indicated by a dot either above or below the note head.

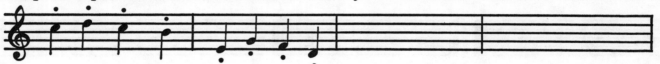

4. A FERMATA (fer-MAH-tah) or hold sign is used to hold a note longer than its original value. The note is usually held about twice its time value. Often, the Fermata is referred to as a "Hold" or "Bird's Eye."

4. DEFINE THE DYNAMICS   (VIII–4)

DYNAMICS is a term meaning the degree of loudness or softness in which music is played or sung. The most common Dynamics in use are listed in the following chart.

Draw the symbols so they match the printed ones. Then solve the definitions by decoding the answers. The definition is given as a mirrored reflection.

	Pronunciation and Symbol Name	Symbol	Draw the Symbol	Reflected Answer	Definition
1.	(pee-ann-ISS-im-oh) Pianissimo	*pp*		yrev tfos	
2.	(MET-so) Mezzo Piano	*mp*		yletaredom tfos	
3.	Piano	*p*		tfos	
4.	(MET-so FOR-tay) Mezzo Forte	*mf*		yletaredom duol	
5.	(FOR-tay) Forte	*f*		duol	
6.	(for-TISS-im-moe) Fortissimo	*ff*		yrev duol	
7.	(Kree-SHEN-doe) Crescendo	*cresc.*		worg reduol	
8.	Diminuendo or Decrescendo	*decresc.* or *dim.*		worg retfos	

Use the symbols in the chart to match the definitions below. Draw the symbols above the staff lines at the beginning of the following measures.

9. Measure 1 – soft
10. Measure 2 – louder
11. Measure 4 – moderately loud
12. Measure 5 – very loud

13. Measure 6 – grow softer
14. Measure 7 – moderately soft
15. Measure 8 – very soft

"Relaxin' "

A. Adair

5. MATCH THE TEMPO   (VIII–5)

TEMPO is the rate of speed music is played or sung. TEMPO MARKINGS are words and symbols used for indicating the rate of speed.

How good is your Italian? Unscramble the English translation for these Tempo terms. Write your answers on the blanks. The first one is done for you.

1. Largo (LAHR-go)
   revy llwosy___very slowly___

2. Lento (LEN-toe)
   llwosy _____

3. Adagio (ad-DAH-jee-oh)
   llwosy, lelirusey_____

4. Andante (ann-DAHN-tay)
   lkwangi acpe _____

5. Moderato (mod-er-RAH-toe)
   mdrtlyeaeo _____

6. Allegretto (ah-lahg-GRET-doe)
   cquikly_____

7. Allegro (ah-LAY-grow)
   yleivly_____

8. Vivace (vee-VAH-chay)
   yleivly_____

9. Presto (PRESS-toe)
   revy staf_____

10. Prestissimo (press-TISS-i-mo)
    sterfa hant "Pertso"_____

From the list above, match a Tempo Marking with each of the songs below. Write the number of the Tempo Marking on the blank.

_____11. Brahms' "Lullaby"
_____12. "Summertime" from *Porgy and Bess* by George Gershwin
_____13. "Stars and Stripes Forever" by John Philip Sousa
_____14. "America the Beautiful," words by Katherine Lee Bates
_____15. "Flight of the Bumble Bee" by Rimski-Korsakov

The following terms all mean a change in tempo.

ACCELERANDO (*accel.*) to become faster   RITARDANDO (*rit.*) becoming slower
RALLENTANDO (*rall.*) gradually slowing   RITENUTO (*riten.*) immediate slowing
                      in speed

A TEMPO (*a tempo*) means to resume the original tempo.

16. Underline the Tempo Markings in the tune below.

You may need to do some research to find the answers to the next two questions.

17. What is the purpose of a METRONOME? _____

_____

18. Who was Mälzel (Maelzel)? _____

_____

Name _____   Score _____

Date _____   Class _____

6. *SCRAMBLED SYMBOLS*   *(VIII–6)*

Listed below are several categories of scrambled music terms. How
many of these music terms can you unscramble? Write the terms and
their definitions on the blanks.

TEMPO: Indicates rate of speed

_____ 1. ragoL _____

_____ 2. gadAoi _____

_____ 3. Moertado _____

_____ 4. llgroeA _____

           Changing tempos

_____ 5. onrlecAcdae _____

_____ 6. A epomt _____

_____ 7. itr. _____

DYNAMICS: the volume of sound

_____ 8. iPaon _____

_____ 9. Fetor _____

STYLE: The character or mood of the composition

_____10. geLtao _____

_____11. catoctaS _____

MISCELLANEOUS TERMS

_____12. D.C. la iFne _____

_____13. mataFer _____

_____14. C.D. _____

_____15. ineF _____

7. USE SYMBOL SENSE   (VIII–7)

Circle the correct answer.

1. Which shows the longest duration?	**o** a.	♩ b.	♪(half) c.
2. Which shows the softest?	*f* a.	*ff* b.	*pp* c.
3. Which rest is the longest?	a.	b.	c.
4. Which means "to grow louder"?	*staccato* a.	*cresc* b.	*decresc.* c.
5. Which shows the shortest duration?	♩(half) a.	♪ b.	♩ c.
6. Which means "become slower"?	*rit* a.	*accel.* b.	*a tempo* c

Name _____   Score _____

Date _____   Class _____

8. DRAW THE SYMBOL   (VIII—8)

Draw the symbol to match the word in the box.

	1.	2.	3.	4.
	STAFF	TREBLE CLEF	QUARTER NOTE	HALF NOTE
	5.	6.	7.	8.
	WHOLE NOTE	EIGHTH NOTE	MEASURE	REPEAT SIGN
	9.	10.	11.	12.
	DOUBLE BAR LINE	SOFT	LOUD	FERMATA
	13.	14.	15.	16.
	BAR LINE	TIME SIGNATURE	BASS CLEF	FLAT
	17.	18.	19.	20.
	SHARP	QUARTER REST	HALF REST	WHOLE REST
	21.	22.	23.	24.
	EIGHTH REST	NATURAL	ACCENT	VERY LOUD

Name _____   Score _____

Date _____   Class _____

9. THE SECRET SCRAMBLE

Unscramble the music terms and write them on the blanks. The definition for each term is given to provide you a clue.

_____ 1. L D O H   A sign indicating that a note or rest is to be held longer than usual.

_____ 2. P E E R A T   A sign indicating that certain measures are to be sung or played again.

_____ 3. E T I   A curved line connecting two notes of the same pitch. The notes are sung or played as one tone and not repeated.

_____ 4. L S R U   A curved line connecting notes of different pitch. These notes are to be sung or played without a break in sound.

_____ 5. E L O H W   T O N E   The longest note commonly used in music.

_____ 6. F L A H   T O E N   A symbol of music duration; half the time of a whole note.

_____ 7. R A U T R E Q   T E O N   A note that is filled in and has a stem.

_____ 8. F A S T F   The five lines and spaces on which notes are written.

_____ 9. S U R E E A M   The distance between two bar lines.

_____ 10. L A F T   A sign that lowers a tone by one-half step.

_____ 11. H A R P S   A sign that raises a tone by one-half step.

_____ 12. L O O S   When one person performs alone.

_____ 13. T U E D   When two people perform as a group.

_____ 14. R I T O   When three people perform as a group.

10. FIND THE HIDDEN MESSAGE   (VIII–10)

Below are pairs of words. Read them over before you begin. You will note that some pairs are alike in meaning, while others are opposites. If the words are alike, place an "X" in the box below "Alike." If the words are opposite in meaning, place an "X" in the box below "Opposite." Clue: When you are finished, the letters not crossed out will spell a sentence. Write the sentence at the bottom of the page.

#	ALIKE	OPPOSITE		#	ALIKE	OPPOSITE	
1.	B	E	rest – silent	18.	B	A	pitch – tone
2.	A	V	legato – staccato	19.	A	V	blues – jazz
3.	C	E	bass clef – treble clef	20.	N	E	coda – "tail"
4.	H	N	piccolo – contra bassoon	21.	D	R	presto – fast
5.	A	I	beat – count	22.	Y	I	minor – major
6.	M	N	accent – stress	23.	U	S	refrain – chorus
7.	S	O	accompaniment – a cappella	24.	P	A	piano – forte
8.	U	T	accidental – alteration	25.	I	E	trio – three
9.	R	I	sharp – flat	26.	C	A	bass – treble
10.	E	U	tempo – speed	27.	I	T	adagio – allegro
11.	T	M	bar – measure	28.	A	S	alto – soprano
12.	O	E	baton – stick	29.	L	O	band – chorus
13.	N	O	coda – introduction	30.	A	S	meter – time
14.	E	T	keyboard – piano	31.	H	O	fermata – hold
15.	B	H	kettle drum – tympani	32.	U	A	solo – ensemble
16.	O	A	tune – melody	33.	M	N	pizzicato – pluck
17.	W	S	duo –duet	34.	E	D	autoharp – chromoharp

11. A SYMBOL CROSSWORD PUZZLE   (VIII–11)

ACROSS

2. ♭

4. 𝄾   _____ rest

6. ♩↗

8. ▬   _____ rest

11. 𝄫   _____ bar

12. ⏜

14. *p*

16. D.C.   _____ Capo

17. 𝄐

18. 𝄢

DOWN

1. ♪↗

3. ♫

5. ▬   _____ rest

7. 𝄞   _____ Clef

9. :∥   _____ sign

10. 𝄾   _____ rest

13. ▬▬▬

14. 𝅝   _____ note

15. ♭♭   double _____

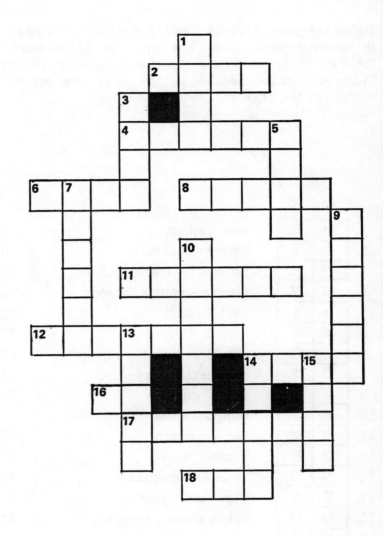

Name _____

Date _____

12. THE SYMBOL SEARCH   (VIII–12)

How many symbols can you locate in this song?

1. Draw a line under the Treble Clef signs.
2. Circle the chord letters.
3. Draw an arrow under the Meter Signature.
4. Draw a rectangle over the dotted half notes.
5. Draw an "X" where the song ends.
6. Trace over the ties.
7. Draw a square below the sharps in the key signature.
8. Draw a triangle on the accent mark.

"Looby Loo"

Quickly   English Song

Here we go loo - by   loo,   Here we go loo - by   light,

Here we go loo - by   loo,   All on a Sat-ur-day   night.

I   put my right   hand   in,   I   take my right hand

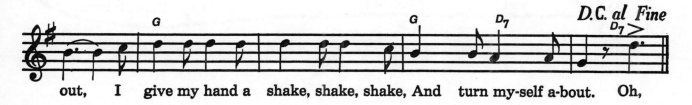

out,   I   give my hand a   shake, shake, shake, And   turn my-self a-bout.   Oh,

2. left hand	4. left foot	6. whole self
3. right foot	5. big head	

Name _____   Score _____

Date _____   Class _____

13. CAN YOU WIN?

You are a race car driver. Your job is to see how fast you can make it to the end of the raceway. Each section of the road has four words—three are alike in some way and one is different. Draw a line through the one that is different. When you get to the finish line, use the back of this paper to draw a picture of your race car.

START HERE

1. march
   spiritual
   banjo
   jazz

2. half
   quarter
   rest
   whole

3. loud
   fast
   slow
   moderato

4. pianissimo
   melody
   crescendo
   forte

5. duet
   quartet
   solo
   drum

6. clarinet
   tenor
   flute
   bassoon

7. saxophone
   bass
   alto
   soprano

8. pick
   neck
   strings
   voice

9. interval
   band
   orchestra
   symphony

10. Strauss
    Tchaikovsky
    Brahms
    Picasso

11. La
    Fa
    To
    Re

12. fermata
    fine
    bird's eye
    hold

13. round
    pulse
    beat
    count

14. polka
    waltz
    anchovies
    disco

15. do
    keynote
    home town
    tonal center

16. legato
    smooth
    staccato
    flowing

17. contrabassoon
    castanets
    bass clarinet
    English horn

18. slow
    ff
    fortissimo
    very loud

19. choir
    chorus
    vocal ensemble
    bass clef

20. sharp
    natural
    accident
    flat

FINISH

14. SOLVE THE SECRET SCRIPT   (VIII–14)

Match the definitions with the terms by writing the letters for the definitions on the blanks. The first one is done for you. (Some letters are used more than once.)

_T_	1.	REPEAT SIGN	(E)	the loudness or softness of a pitch
____	2.	MEASURE	(E)	the distance between two bar lines
____	3.	STAFF	(R)	the five lines with spaces used for music notation
____	4.	TREBLE CLEF	(E)	the highness or lowness of a tone
____	5.	PITCH	(S)	the length of time a note is held
____	6.	DURATION	(T)	a series of tones arranged in a special order
____	7.	INTENSITY	(H)	the quality of a tone
____	8.	TIMBRE	(N)	a member of the woodwind family
____	9.	WHOLE NOTE	(T)	a member of the percussion family
____	10.	HALF NOTE	(L)	♩
____	11.	QUARTER NOTE	(O)	a member of the string family
____	12.	EIGHTH NOTE	(T)	
____	13.	SCALE	(D)	a member of the brass family
____	14.	TYMPANI	(L)	♩
____	15.	FLUTE	(T)	𝅝
____	16.	DOUBLE BASS	(E)	♪
____	17.	FRENCH HORN	(C)	

Solve the secret script by writing the message below.

Don't monkey around! The title of this activity is your clue to the answer.

15. JOIN THE MUSICAL MARATHON

How far can you run? Keep adding two more miles for each definition you write. Each music term on the track has two meanings. When you complete all the meanings, you get the last two miles and 385 yards as a bonus. Can you finish the 26-mile 385-yard marathon? Good luck!

START HERE!

Music Definition   1.   Other Definition
REFRAIN
4 mi.   2 mi.

Music Definition   2.   Other Definition
TIE
6 mi.   8 mi.

Music Definition   3.   Other Definition
KEY
12 mi.   10 mi.

Music Definition   4.   Other Definition
PITCH
14 mi.   16 mi.

Music Definition   5.   Other Definition
METER
20 mi.   18 mi.

Music Definition   6.   Other Definition
REST
22 mi.

FINISH
26 mi.
385 yds.

When you complete the race, draw a picture of yourself at the finish line.

16. A "SYMBOL" QUIZ   (VIII–16)

Choose the correct answer and underline the letter.

1. The three parts that make up a note are the flag, the head and the __.
       a. stick   b. stem   c. beat

2. The note heads of whole and half notes are __ filled in.
       a. always   b. sometimes   c. never

3. The only note that does not have a stem is the __.
       a. half note   b. quarter note   c. whole note

4. The eighth note and notes of shorter duration (length) have __ in common.
       a. flags   b. sixteenth   c. speed

5. A flag added to the stem of a note decreases the duration by __.
       a. $\frac{1}{4}$ b. $\frac{1}{8}$ c. $\frac{1}{2}$

6. Silent beats in music are called __.
       a. pauses   b. rests   c. stops

7. Music is written on a __.
       a. measure   b. treble clef   c. staff

8. When two or more eighth notes are grouped together, the heavy line called a __ may be used in place of flags.
       a. beam   b. rod   c. stem

9. For notes with more than one flag, an __ number of beams must be used to replace the flags.
       a. unequal   b. odd   c. equal

10. The distance between bar lines is called a __.
       a. staff   b. clef   c. measure

11. The double bar lines mean the __ of a song.
       a. end   b. introduction   c. finale

12. The symbol used at the beginning of the staff to indicate the upper half of the keyboard is the __.
       a. bass clef   b. treble clef   c. minor scale

13. The stems of the note should be __ space(s) high.
       a. 3   b. 5   c. 1

14. There are __ lines on the staff.
       a. 4   b. 8   c. 5

TEACHER'S GUIDE
AND ANSWER KEY

1. Uncover the Clue

1. Staff	6. Tempo	11. Quarter Note	16. Flat
2. Notes	7. Beat	12. Whole Note	17. Keynote
3. Pitch	8. Line Note	13. Sharp	18. Degrees
4. Treble Clef	9. Space Note	14. Interval	19. Natural
5. Leger Lines	10. Face	15. Rest	20. Meter

2. Draw the Symbols

Students might be interested in pronouncing the term "Da capo," which means repeat from the beginning. Another Italian music term you might introduce along with "Fine" is "Dal segno." Dal segno (dahl SAY-no) means: Go back to the sign 𝄋 (abbreviation: D.S.). D.S. al fine (FEE-nay) means go back to the sign 𝄋 and play until "Fine."

3. Label the Symbols

Play examples of the TIE, SLUR, STACCATO and FERMATA. Use an instrument such as a piano or recorder. After students are familiar with the sound of each, let them guess which example you are playing.

4. Define the Dynamics

1. very soft	5. loud	9. *p*	13. *decresc.* ⟩
2. moderately soft	6. very loud	10. *f*	14. *mp*
3. soft	7. grow louder	11. *mf*	15. *pp*
4. moderately loud	8. grow softer	12. *ff*	

5. Match the Tempo

1. very slowly	6. quickly	11. 2	Answers may vary for
2. slowly	7. lively	12. 3	questions 11–15.
3. slowly, leisurely	8. lively	13. 6	
4. walking pace	9. very fast	14. 5	
5. moderately	10. faster than Presto	15. 8	

16. *accel.*   *a tempo*   *rit.*

17. The metronome is a mechanical instrument to indicate the exact speed in music. It may be adjusted to tick the number of beats per minute. M.M. ♩ = 80 means the speed is 80 quarter notes per minute.

18. He invented the metronome.

6. Scrambled Symbols

1. Largo – very slowly
2. Adagio – slowly
3. Moderato – moderately
4. Allegro – lively
5. Accelerando – to become faster
6. A tempo – resume original tempo
7. rit. – become slower
8. Piano – soft
9. Forte – loud
10. Legato – smoothly
11. Staccato – disconnected tones
12. D.C. al Fine – repeat from the beginning
13. Fermata – pause, or hold the note
14. C.D. – (Da capo) go to the beginning
15. Fine – the end

7. Use Symbol Sense

1. a
2. c
3. c
4. b
5. b
6. a

8. Draw the Symbol

Number the symbols from 1 – 28 beginning with the accent mark at the top to the last eighth note on the bottom of the page. Use those numbers as the answers.

1. 9	7. 9	13. 9	19. 7
2. 26	8. 3	14. 13, 14 or 18	20. 12
3. 17	9. 23	15. 20	21. 6 or 15
4. 19	10. 22	16. 25	22. 8
5. 5	11. 10	17. 21	23. 1
6. 27 or 28	12. 2 or 16	18. 24	24. 11

9. The Secret Scramble

Introduce the following terms in preparation for questions 12, 13 and 14:

Solo – music for one performer
Duet – music for two performers
Trio – music for three performers

1. HOLD	5. WHOLE NOTE	9. MEASURE	13. DUET
2. REPEAT	6. HALF NOTE	10. FLAT	14. TRIO
3. TIE	7. QUARTER NOTE	11. SHARP	
4. SLUR	8. STAFF	12. SOLO	

10. Find the Hidden Message

* You may need to review words like "baton," "jazz," and "autoharp."

The letters that are not crossed out spell: "Each instrument has a very special sound."

11. A Symbols Crossword Puzzle

12. The Symbol Search

"Here We Go Looby Loo"

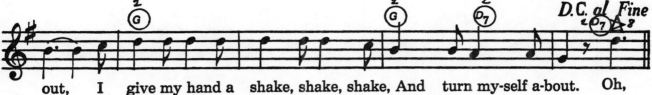

I put my right hand in, I take my right hand out, I give my hand a shake, shake, shake, And turn my-self a-bout. Oh,

* Students might form a circle and perform the motions described in the song. For an autoharp accompaniment, use the following chords: $I = G$, $V_7 = D_7$.

Note: This song does not use any sharps in the melody line.

13. Can You Win?

1. banjo	6. tenor	11. To	16. staccato
2. rest	7. saxophone	12. fine	17. castanets
3. loud	8. voice	13. round	18. slow
4. melody	9. interval	14. anchovies	19. bass clef
5. drum	10. Picasso	15. home town	20. accident

14. Solve the Secret Script

The answer reads backwards from number 17 to number 1: "Don't tell the secret."

15. Join the Musical Marathon

	Music Definition	Other Definition
REFRAIN:	A phrase or verse repeated regularly in a song; also called a chorus.	To hold oneself back; abstain.
TIE:	A curved line drawn above or below notes that are to be played or sung continuously.	To fasten with a string; join or connect.
KEY:	Scale of notes; one of a set of parts pressed on the piano.	A device that locks and unlocks.
PITCH:	The degree of highness or lowness of a sound.	Throw, toss; slope.
METER:	Same as Time Signature.	A device for measuring.
REST:	A mark in music to show a silent beat, a pause.	To sleep, be still; what is left.

16. A "Symbol" Quiz

1. b	3. c	5. c	7. c	9. c	11. a	13. a
2. c	4. a	6. b	8. a	10. c	12. b	14. c

Section IX
BE A COMPOSER

No.	Activity Title	Skill Involved
1.	A MUSICAL WORD RACE	(Creating words from notes)
2.	RESCUE MR. C. MORENOTES	(Correcting a tune)
3.	FIND THE MUSICAL ORDER	(Numbering measures to rewrite a tune)
4.	FIND THE ERRORS	(Correcting a tune)
5.	REWRITE THE TUNE	(Rewriting a rhythm pattern with different notes)
6.	DO IT DIFFERENTLY	(Adding a measure with different rhythm)
7.	QUESTION + ANSWER = PERIOD	(Identifying phrases)
8.	CAN I COMPOSE?	(Constructing a melody)

TEACHER'S GUIDE AND ANSWER KEY

1. A MUSICAL WORD RACE

(IX–1)

Win this race by making as many words as you can from the Musical Alphabet: A B C D E F G.

Write as many words as you can think of and draw the matching notes on the staff. The first one is done to show you how.

1. _G A G E_ 2. _____ 3. _____ 4. _____

5. _____ 6. _____ 7. _____ 8. _____

9. _____ 10. _____ 11. _____ 12. _____

13. _____ 14. _____ 15. _____ 16. _____

17. _____ 18. _____ 19. _____ 20. _____

Name _____ Score _____

Date _____ Class _____

2. *RESCUE MR. C. MORENOTES*

Mr. C. Morenotes needs your help. He needs you to finish some details to this composition so that he can meet his deadline. While rewriting this song, Mr. C. Morenotes was a bit absent-minded. Please read the directions below so you can finish the song.

1. Add the missing Treble Clef at the beginning of the second staff.
2. Finish numbering the measures for the song.
3. Add the missing flat in the Key Signature on the second staff.
4. Complete measure two to make it look like measure one.
5. Complete measure four to make it look like measure three.
6. Complete measure six to make it look like measure five.
7. Complete measure eight to make it look like measure seven.
8. Draw a double bar at the end of the song.
9. Add the missing number for the Meter Signature.
10. Write the title of this well-known song on the space below.

_____

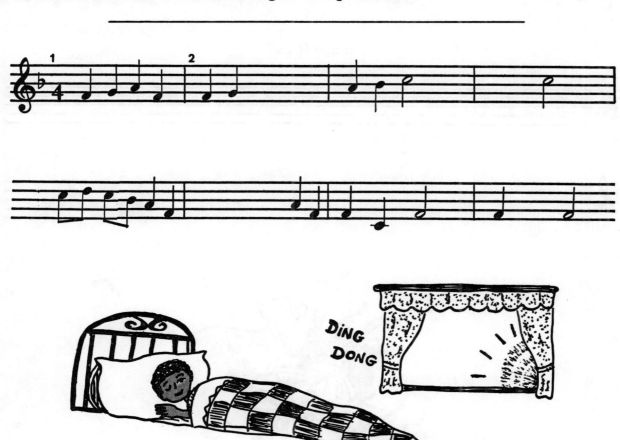

Name _____   Score _____

Date _____   Class _____

3. FIND THE MUSICAL ORDER   (IX-3)

The measures in this song got mixed up and are in the wrong order. Measure number 1 is the only measure in the right place. Number the rest of the measures to show the correct order. After the measures are numbered, rewrite the song on the staff below.

"Jingle Bells"

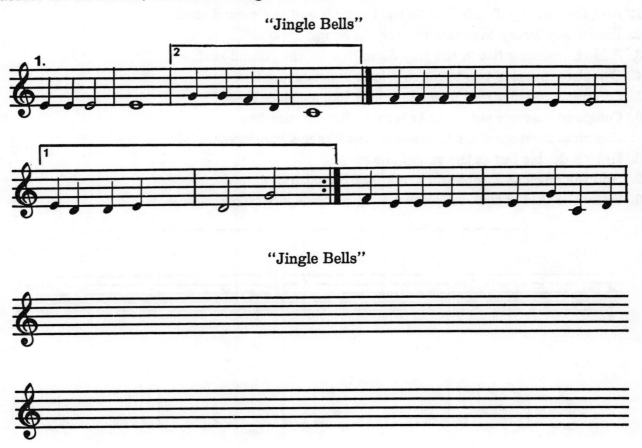

"Jingle Bells"

4. FIND THE ERRORS   (IX–4)

Are you a good detective? In this song there are 15 items that need correcting. When you discover the mistakes, change them on the musical score by making the corrections on the staff.

"America"

Name _____ Score _____

Date _____ Class _____

5. REWRITE THE TUNE (IX–5)

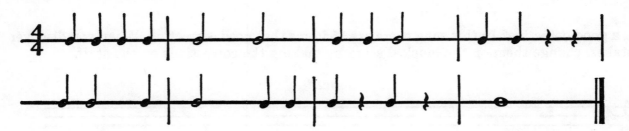

Rewrite this rhythm pattern using "F" space notes on the staff below. The first measure is done to show you how.

1.

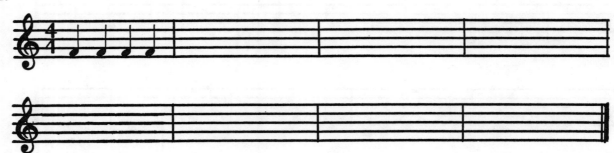

Rewrite the above rhythm pattern, beginning on "Low C" and using neighboring notes or repeated notes. Write the letter names under the notes.

2.

Name _____   Score _____

Date _____   Class _____

6. DO IT DIFFERENTLY   (IX–6)

Finish the last measure in each phrase by adding a different rhythm pattern from the first three. The first one is done to show you how.

1.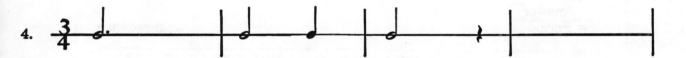

2.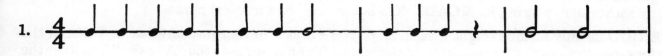

3.

4.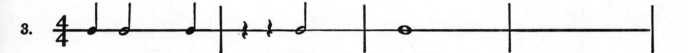

5.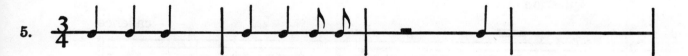

6.

7.

8.

7. QUESTION + ANSWER = PERIOD   (IX–7)

A PHRASE is part of a musical sentence. PHRASES are usually found in regular groupings of four or eight measures. Think of taking a "breath" at the end of each phrase as if you were singing the melody rather than playing it. A CADENCE is the close of a musical phrase.

A PERIOD usually includes eight measures, or two Phrases of four measures each. Think of the first four measures as the "Question" and the second four measures as the "Answer." Together the eight measures make a period. Two eight-measure periods, as in this song, equal a DOUBLE PERIOD.

"Theme from Beethoven's Ninth Symphony"

Answer the following questions by filling in the blanks.

1. What do we call two phrases of four measures each? _____

2. The question phrase ends with a semi-cadence on an accented beat in the fourth measure. That note belongs to the V chord. In this case, what is that note in measure 4? _____

3. What are the notes in the V chord in the Key of G Major? _____

4. The answer phrase usually begins on the same beat as the question phrase. What is the beat on which the phrase begins in measure 5? _____

5. The answer phrase usually ends on an accented note and on the keynote of the scale. What is the keynote of the scale for this song? _____

6. What is the letter name of the accented note at the end of the answer phrase in measure 16? _____

8. CAN I COMPOSE?   (IX–8)

"March in Time"
Lift your feet up, march in time!
Lift your feet up, march in time!
Better every season, Better do it fine.
Lift your feet up, march in time!

Use this procedure to write your song:

1. Decide what type of mood this poem expresses. Is there anything that may reflect a descending or ascending pattern in pitch?
2. Read the poem again and decide a definite rhythm pattern. Clap the rhythm.
3. Underline the heavily accented words or syllables.
4. Draw bar lines to the left side of the heavily accented words and/or syllables.
5. Decide on the rhythm pattern and melody for the first phrase (sentence) and notate it on the staff. Proceed phrase by phrase. Some composers learn to write very rapidly by using little lines (/), then filling in the notes and rhythms later.
6. Draw the bar lines to the left of the heavily accented notes on the staff.
7. Decide what the Key Signature and Meter Signature will be, and add dynamic markings.
8. Write the words to the poem below the staff lines. Carefully line up each word with the matching note.

"March in Time"

TEACHER'S GUIDE
AND ANSWER KEY

1. A Musical Race

Suggested answers:

age	bad	cage	dab	fed
aged	badge	cab	gab	feed
add	bag	cabbage	egg	fade
added	beg	cafe	edge	
ace	bed	dad	face	
baggage	bead	dead	fad	

2. Rescue Mr. C. Morenotes

"Are You Sleeping?"

3. Find the Musical Order

4. Find the Errors

5. Rewrite the Tune

Answers will vary.

6. Do It Differently

Answers will vary.

7. Question + Answer = Period

Play a recording of Beethoven's "Ninth Symphony."

1. period
2. A
3. D – F sharp – A
4. 1
5. G
6. G

8. Can I Compose?

* As soon as children can use notation, create a song on the chalkboard using notation. Select a short, simple poem, or ask the children to make up a poem. Encourage classroom participation and use the guidelines described in IX-8.
* Chords: Use one of the student's songs to decide which chords are suitable. Notate the chords and play on an autoharp.

Section X
LEARNING TO LISTEN

Name _____   Score _____

Date _____   Class _____

1. YOUR OPINION, PLEASE   (X–1)

1. What does music appreciation mean to you? _____
   _____
   _____

2. How can you keep from being a passive listener? _____
   _____

3. How do you use music in your leisure time? _____
   _____

4. How might music help maintain one's composure? _____
   _____

5. In what way, if possible, can music help develop a normal well-balanced individual? _____
   _____
   _____

6. How can music be used to broaden your interests? _____
   _____

7. How do you feel about the following idea? Popular music can be listened to at any time, it doesn't last (have permanence) and because there is such a wide choice of numbers to listen to, popular music should be avoided in music class. _____
   _____

8. What does the phrase "learn to listen then listen to learn" mean to you? _____
   _____

9. How do you think your appreciation of music will change as you grow older? _____
   _____

10. What new areas of music would you be interested in listening to (for example: opera, ballet, classical, musicals, etc.)? _____
    _____

2. HOW DO YOU LISTEN? (X-2)

1. What type of music do you prefer? Why? _____
   _____

2. What things in your environment might you control to help you concentrate more on listening
   to music? _____
   _____

3. List four ways that will help you be a more attentive listener.
   a. _____
   b. _____
   c. _____
   d. _____

4. What makes people enjoy familiar music? _____
   _____

5. What benefit is there in hearing a piece of music more than once? _____
   _____

6. What does "standard repertoire" mean? _____
   _____

7. Why is there always standard repertoire music performed at most symphony concerts?
   _____

8. Why is it difficult to make a judgment about a piece of music or a type of music you have
   never heard? _____

Name _____   Score _____

Date _____   Class _____

3. *BROADEN YOUR APPRECIATION* (X-3)

1. How does learning more about the composer help you when listening to his or her music? _____

   _____

2. How do music prejudices limit one from fully enjoying music? _____

   _____

3. To truly appreciate music, do you have to be able to participate yourself? Give a reason for

   your answer. _____

   _____

4. How can you compare the experience of listening to a piece of music to examining a piece of

   art work at a museum? _____

   _____

5. What is musical memory and how is it important to your musical appreciation? _____

   _____

6. Why do you think some people enjoy following a musical score when they listen to music? ____

   _____

   _____

7. Why must you have some understanding of music to enjoy it to the fullest? _____

   _____

8. What type of performances can you attend in your community to broaden your music

   appreciation? _____

Name _____   Score _____

Date _____   Class _____

4. *WHAT'S YOUR ATTITUDE?*   (X–4)

What is your attitude when you're listening to music? Evaluate whether you just hear the music or actually listen to it. Write the word PASSIVE if you are just hearing the music and not really listening. Write the word ACTIVE if you are actually listening to it.

_____ 1. rock concert

_____ 2. music in a restaurant

_____ 3. attending a jazz concert

_____ 4. the stereo at home

_____ 5. radio at home

_____ 6. symphony concert

_____ 7. choir at church

_____ 8. car radio

_____ 9. music over intercom in dentist's or doctor's office

_____ 10. marching band at football game

_____ 11. music lesson

_____ 12. movie

_____ 13. music class in school

_____ 14. a musical

_____ 15. an opera or operetta

_____ 16. a ballet performance

_____ 17. a recording at the music store

_____ 18. watching television

TEACHER'S GUIDE
AND ANSWER KEY

* Discuss how we are continually exposed to music of all kinds. (Music sells products, creates atmosphere in restaurants, and provides background in stores, doctors' and dentists' offices. We hear music in nature.) How does television use music?

* Discuss how music is a part of family life and how it brings people together. Do members of the family sing together? Does anyone play an instrument or sing in a choir or musical group? What type of music do the students listen to on their radios and record players? Do the students take advantage of the National Public Radio station or the educational television channel for special music programs? Are your students encouraged to attend concerts?

* Promote live listening in your classroom. If possible, take a field trip to a local junior high or high school to observe a band, orchestra or choir concert or a rehearsal. Encourage local musicians to perform for your class to explain and demonstrate their instruments.

* Show enthusiasm and listen attentively with your class. No special knowledge of music is necessary to foster good listening habits. Encourage your students to express themselves by reacting physically and responding naturally to the movement of music. Help make listening a basic skill by encouraging the students to actively listen for something in the music and always continue to make new discoveries. Listen for melody, rhythm, harmony, instrumentation, contrast, repetition, tempo, and dynamics.

1. *Your Opinion, Please*

   Answers will vary.

2. *How Do You Listen?*

   Answers will vary.

3. *Broaden Your Appreciation*

   Answers will vary.

4. *What's Your Attitude?*

   Answers will vary.

Section XI
TRAINING YOUR EAR

No.	Activity Title	Skill Involved
1.	BASS OR TREBLE?	(Recognizing high and low sounds)
2.	WHAT DO YOU HEAR?	(Hearing sound direction)
3.	LISTEN AND CHECK	(Hearing and recognizing measures)
4.	"RIGHT THEM"	(Rewriting notes in the right order)
5.	LISTEN TO THE BEAT	(Hearing and locating the incorrect measure)
6.	HOW'S YOUR HEARING?	(Hearing which notes are played)
7.	CHOOSE THE PATTERN	(Selecting the correct musical pattern)
8.	DECIDE THE METER	(Conducting and writing the meter)
9.	IDENTIFY THE INTERVALS	(Distinguishing between melodic and harmonic intervals)
10.	CHECK THE SCALES	(Identifying altered notes in Major scales)
11.	PICK THE TUNE	(Recognizing beginning melody patterns)
12.	STEP, SKIP, OR REPEAT?	(Hearing and stating steps, skips, and repeats)
13.	JUDGE THE MUSIC	(Identifying pitch direction on the keyboard)
14.	DRAW THE INSTRUMENT	(Drawing the instrument you hear being played)

TEACHER'S GUIDE AND ANSWER KEY

Note: Use this section in conjunction with the other sections in the book.

Name _____   Score _____

Date _____   Class _____

1. BASS OR TREBLE?   (XI–1)

Music played above "Middle C" is written with the Treble Clef.
Music played lower than "Middle C" is written with the Bass Clef.

You will hear music sounding either higher than "Middle C" or lower
than "Middle C." If the music sounds higher, circle the Treble Clef. If
the music sounds lower, circle the Bass Clef.

1.    2.

3.    4.

For the music you will now hear, draw a Treble Clef if it is played above "Middle C." Draw a Bass
Clef if the music is played below "Middle C."

5.   6.   7.   8.   9.

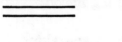

10.   11.   12.   13.   14.

15.   16.   17.   18.   19.

  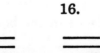

2. WHAT DO YOU HEAR?   (XI–2)

You will hear two tones. Listen carefully. The second tone will be higher, lower, or the same as the first tone. Each example will be played three times. Circle H (higher), L (lower), or S (same) for your answer.

1. H L S   2. H L S   3. H L S   4. H L S   5. H L S   6. H L S
7. H L S   8. H L S   9. H L S   10. H L S   11. H L S   12. H L S

You will now hear two chords. The second will either be the same (S) as the first chord or it will be different (D). Circle the letter that matches your answer. Each chord will be played twice.

13. S D   14. S D   15. S D   16. S D   17. S D   18. S D
19. S D   20. S D   21. S D   22. S D   23. S D   24. S D

Name _____   Score _____

Date _____   Class _____

3. LISTEN AND CHECK   (XI-3)

Each line below has three different rhythm patterns, but only one will be played. Listen carefully to the rhythm. Check the letter that matches the measure you hear. Each example will be played three times.

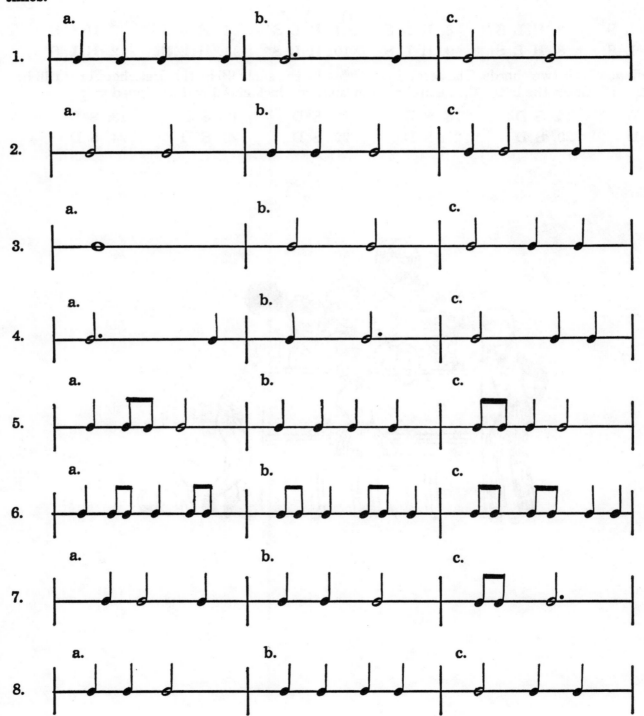

Name _____

Date _____

4. "RIGHT THEM" (XI–4)

The notes on the staffs are in the wrong order. Listen to the patterns being played, and rewrite the notes in the correct order on the staffs.

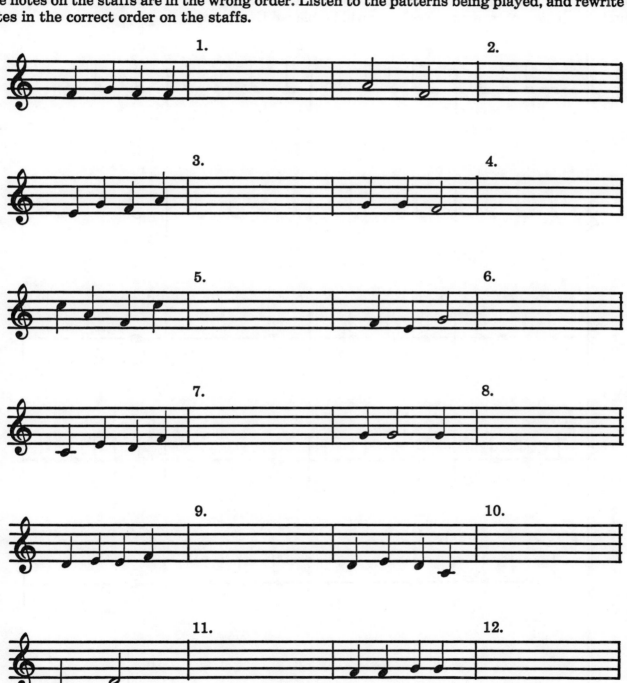

Name ______________________ Score __________

Date ______________________ Class __________

5. LISTEN TO THE BEAT *(XI–5)*

One measure in each group is incorrect. Listen to each example as it is played, and draw an X through the incorrect measure. Each line will be played three times.

a. b. c. d.

1.

a. b. c. d.

2.

a. b. c. d.

3.

a. b. c. d.

4.

a. b. c. d.

5.

a. b. c. d.

6.

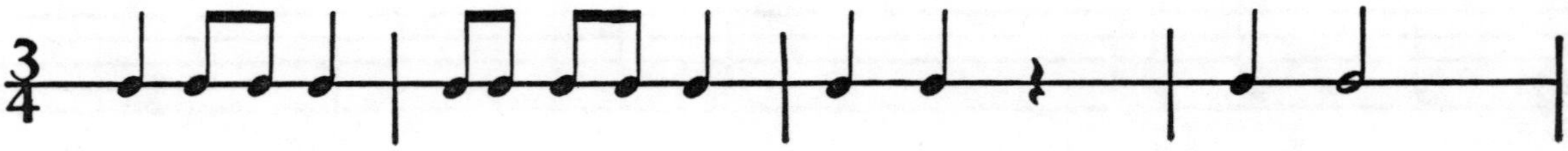

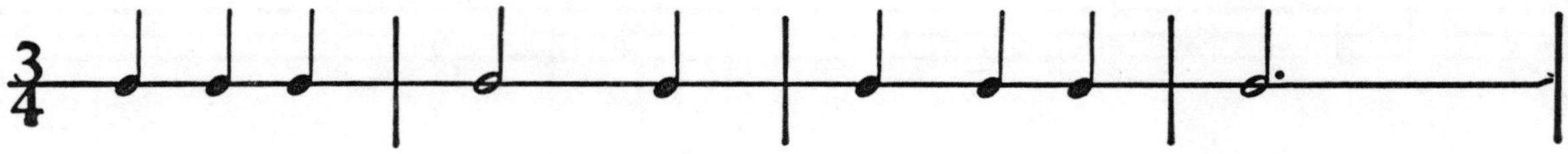

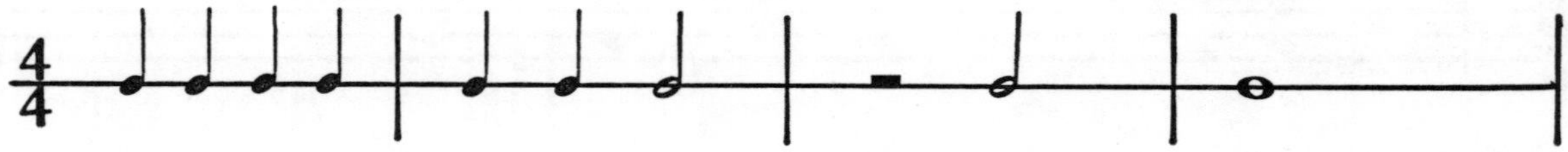

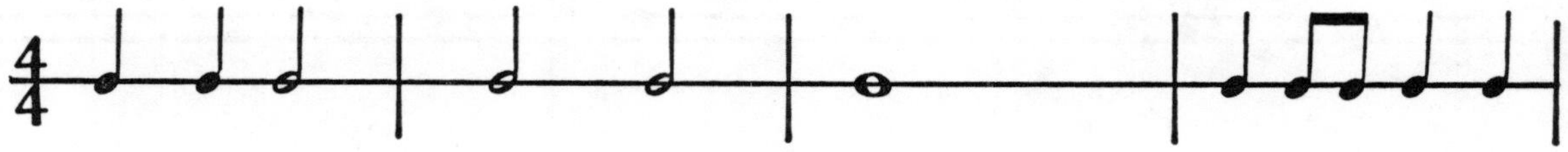

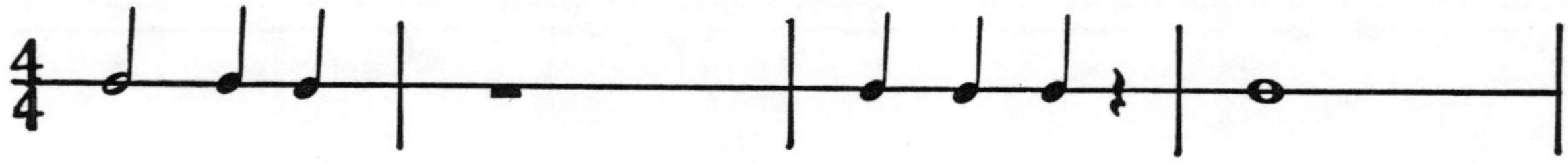

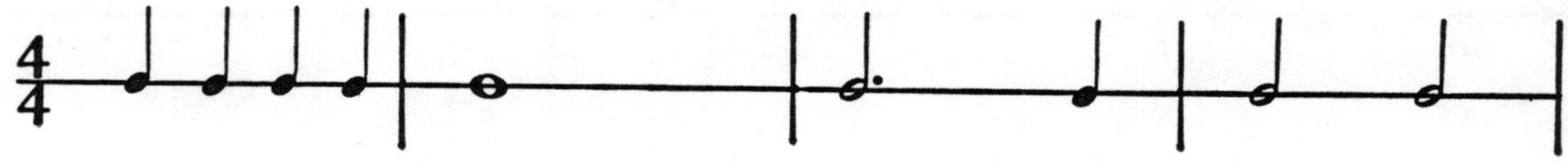

Name _____ Score _____

Date _____ Class _____

6. HOW'S YOUR HEARING? (XI–6)

Listen to each example as it is played three times and draw an X through any note that is played incorrectly.

1.

2.

3.

4.

5.
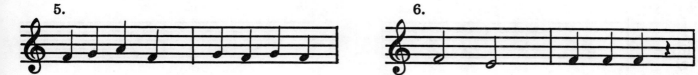

6.

7.

8.

9.

10.
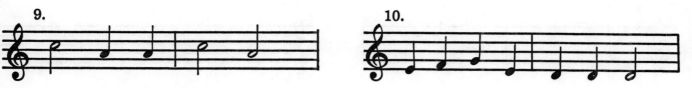

11.

12.

Name _____   Score _____

Date _____   Class _____

7. CHOOSE THE PATTERN

Two musical patterns are given, but only one will be played. Underline the pattern you hear, but be sure to listen carefully before you choose your answer. Each will be played three times.

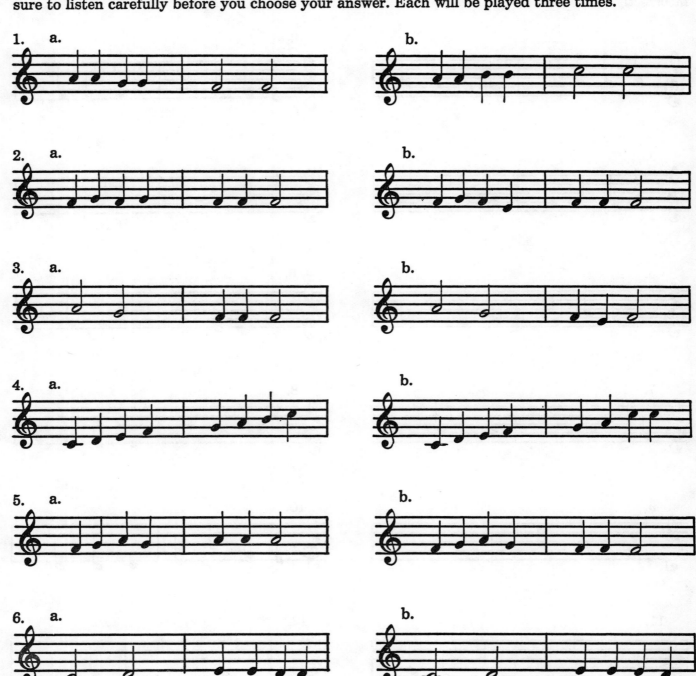

8. DECIDE THE METER   (XI–8)

How can you tell if music swings in two's or three's? As you listen to the examples for this activity, direct your arm to the beat just as a conductor would respond to the music. Move your arm in a downward motion as you hear the accented (loud) beat. Bring your arm up on the beat that is not strong. Use the diagram to help you decide if the music swings in two's (duple meter) or if it swings in three's (triple meter).

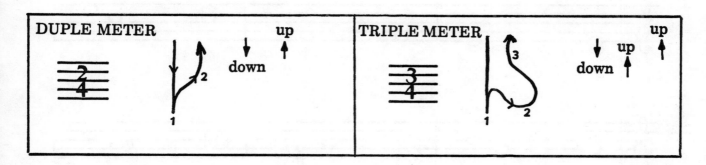

Listen carefully to the music being played for each example. Use your arm to direct and decide whether the meter is in ⅔ or ¾. Then write the Meter Signature on the staff.

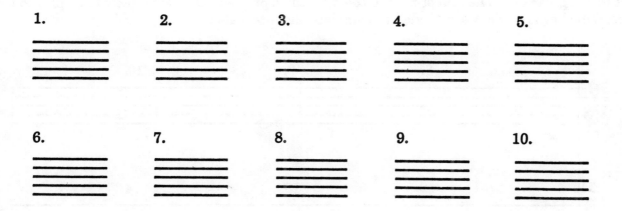

9. IDENTIFY THE INTERVALS   (XI–9)

Two Major Third Intervals are shown in each group, but only one interval will be played. If the two notes are sounded together, circle the Harmonic Interval (in which one note is above the other). If the notes are sounded one after the other, circle the Melodic Interval.

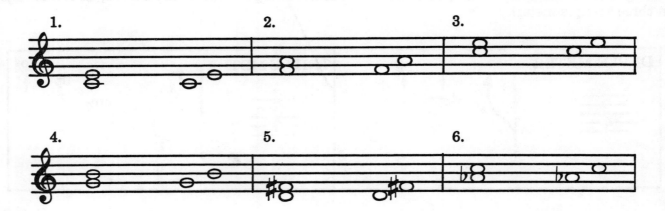

For each of the following, you will hear a Major Third Interval. If it is a Harmonic Interval, draw the second note above the given one. If you hear a Melodic Interval, draw the second note to the right of the given one. The lowest note of the interval is printed. Each example will be played three times. (No sharps or flats are needed to complete the intervals.)

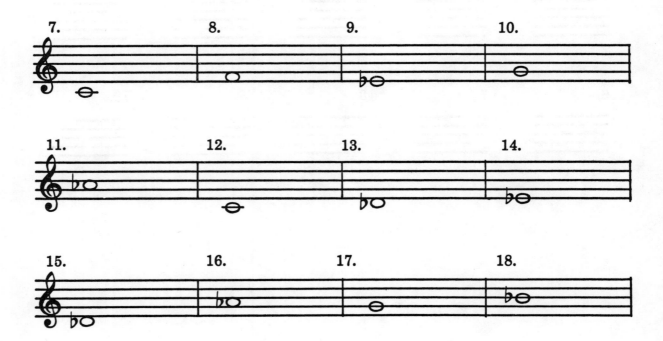

Name _____   Score _____

Date _____   Class _____

10. CHECK THE SCALES   (XI–10)

Below are the letter names for several Major scales. The sharps and flats have been omitted. You are to decide which notes should be altered. Each scale will be played three times. As you listen to the scale, place an X through any note that needs an Accidental. Each scale will first be played as written, then played as it should be.

1. C Major – ascending	C	D	E	F	G	A	B	$\overline{C}$
2. D Major – ascending	D	E	F	G	A	B	$\overline{C}$	$\overline{D}$
3. E Major – ascending	E	F	G	A	B	$\overline{C}$	$\overline{D}$	$\overline{E}$
4. F Major – ascending	F	G	A	B	$\overline{C}$	$\overline{D}$	$\overline{E}$	$\overline{F}$
5. G Major – ascending	G	A	B	$\overline{C}$	$\overline{D}$	$\overline{E}$	$\overline{F}$	$\overline{G}$
6. C Major – descending	$\overline{C}$	B	A	G	F	E	D	C
7. D Major – descending	$\overline{D}$	$\overline{C}$	B	A	G	F	E	D
8. E Major – descending	$\overline{E}$	$\overline{D}$	$\overline{C}$	B	A	G	F	E
9. B Major – ascending	B	C	D	E	F	G	A	B
10. A Major – ascending	A	B	$\overline{C}$	$\overline{D}$	$\overline{E}$	$\overline{F}$	$\overline{G}$	$\overline{A}$

11. PICK THE TUNE   (XI–11)

The following groups of notes illustrate pitch and duration. For each song listed, circle the group of notes that is the best example of how the song begins.

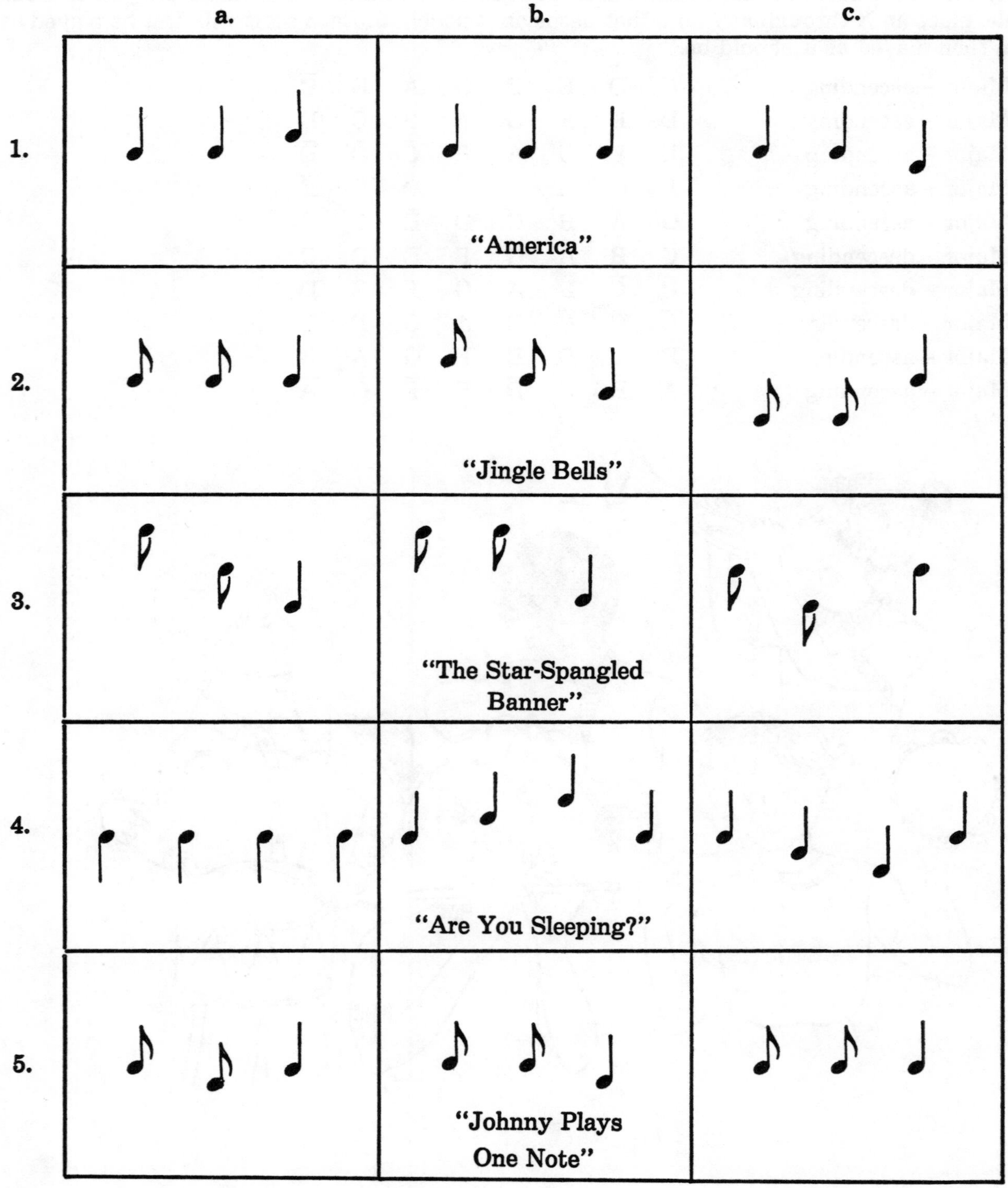

a.   **b.**   **c.**

1.   "America"

2.   "Jingle Bells"

3.   "The Star-Spangled Banner"

4.   "Are You Sleeping?"

5.   "Johnny Plays One Note"

12. STEP, SKIP, OR REPEAT?   (XI–12)

Listen carefully to the notes being played. They may move stepwise, skip a step, or repeat. Mark the direction with an X.

1. STEP____   SKIP____   REPEAT____
2. STEP____   SKIP____   REPEAT____
3. STEP____   SKIP____   REPEAT____
4. STEP____   SKIP____   REPEAT____
5. STEP____   SKIP____   REPEAT____
6. STEP____   SKIP____   REPEAT____
7. STEP____   SKIP____   REPEAT____
8. STEP____   SKIP____   REPEAT____

In the following examples, the second note of each measure is missing. After listening to each pair
of notes being played, decide if the second note moves by step, if it skips a step, or if it repeats
itself. After listening carefully to the interval, draw the second note where it belongs on the staff.

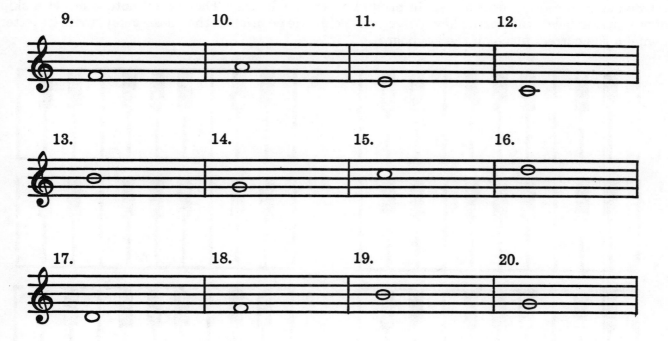

13. JUDGE THE MUSIC   (XI–13)

You will hear two notes being played, one after the other. The letter names of the first notes are printed on the keyboards below. The second note is a neighboring note. You must decide if the second note sounds higher or lower than the first, and then write the letter name of the note on the correct key.

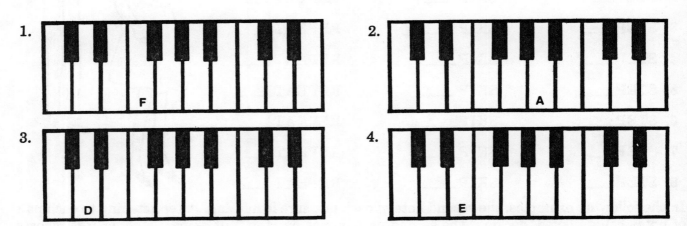

For the following examples, you will again hear two notes being played one after the other. The letter names of the first notes are again printed on the keyboards. The second note is either a skip above or skip below the named key. After you decide the position of the missing key, write its letter name in the correct place on the keyboard.

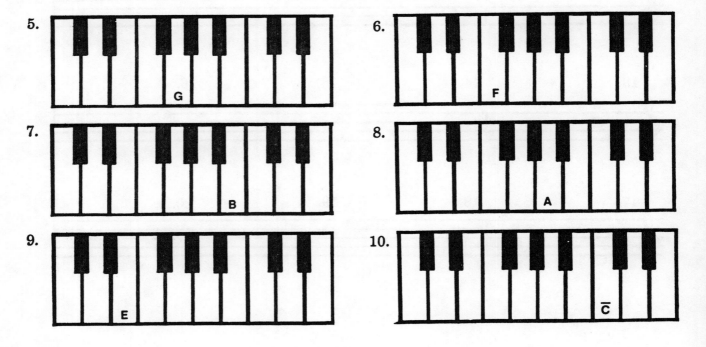

Name _____   Score _____

Date _____   Class _____

14. DRAW THE INSTRUMENT   (XI–14)

Draw the instrument as you hear it being played.

1. FLUTE	2. OBOE	3. BASSOON	4. CLARINET
5. SAXOPHONE	6. TRUMPET	7. TUBA	8. FRENCH HORN
9. SLIDE TROMBONE	10. DOUBLE BASS	11. VIOLIN	12. HARP
13. SNARE DRUM	14. TAMBOURINE	15. CYMBALS	16. TRIANGLE

TEACHER'S GUIDE
AND ANSWER KEY

The activities in this section are designed for the teacher to create his or her own answers. They are intended to be used as follow-up exercises as indicated below.

1. **Bass or Treble?**

   Use with Section I.

2. **What Do You Hear?**

   Use with Section III and/or Section VII.

3. **Listen and Check**

   Use with Section IV and Section V.

   * Determine each rhythm moves in 4's and feel the steady beat. Use these rhythm patterns to make up short melodies.

4. **"Right Them"**

   Use with Sections IV, V and VII.

5. **Listen to the Beat**

   Use with Sections IV and V.

6. **How's Your Hearing?**

   Sample answer: 1. A A A B̸ G G A A
   Use with Sections III and IV.

7. **Choose the Pattern**

   Use with Sections III and IV.

   * Determine all meters are: $\frac{4}{4}$

8. **Decide the Meter**

   Use with Section VI.

9. **Identify the Intervals**

   Use with Section XI.

10. **Check the Scales**

    Use with Section VI.

11. **Pick the Tune**

    1. a   2. a   3. a   4. b   5. c
    Use with Section III.

12. **Step, Skip, or Repeat?**

    Use with Section III or Section VII.

13. **Judge the Music**

    Use with Sections III and VII.

14. **Draw the Instrument**

    Use with Section XIII.

    Listening Suggestion: *Meet the Instruments* (Los Angeles: Bowmar/Noble Publishers, Inc.) includes recordings of each instrument and entire orchestra, along with color charts and filmstrips.

Section XII
TAKING MELODIC DICTATION

Note: This section was designed for use with the other sections of this book.

Name _____   Score _____

Date _____   Class _____

1. FINISH THE RHYTHM PATTERN   (XII–1)

Each rhythm pattern below is missing one measure. Listen carefully as the pattern is played and complete the missing measure. Draw line notes using either quarter notes or half notes.

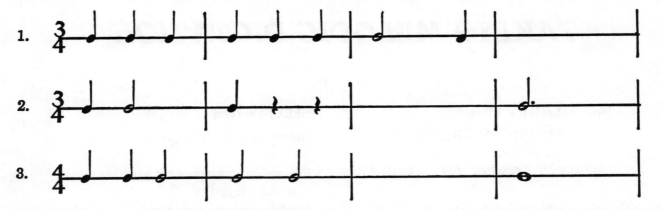

For these rhythm patterns, fill in the missing whole notes and quarter notes to complete the missing measures.

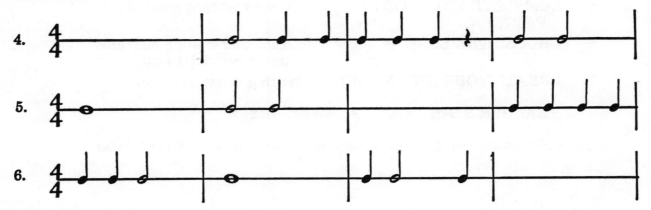

Complete the rhythm patterns below by using either whole notes, half notes, or quarter notes to finish the missing measures.

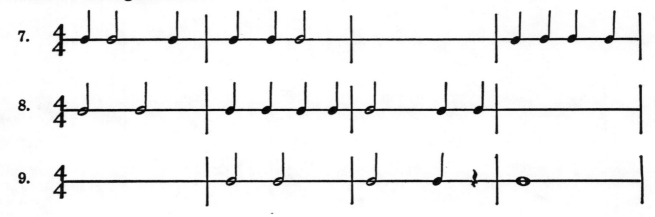

2. RECOGNIZE THE SEQUENCE

There are four measures in each of the following melodies. The first three measures use a short melodic idea that is repeated at different pitch levels. There is only one note in the fourth measure. The first note of measures 1, 2, and 3 is also given. Complete the sequences by writing the notes on different pitch levels as you hear them being played. Each melody will be played three times. The first one is done for you.

Name _____

Date _____

Score _____

Class _____

3. HEAR IT AND WRITE IT

(XII–3)

Follow your teacher's directions for using this page.

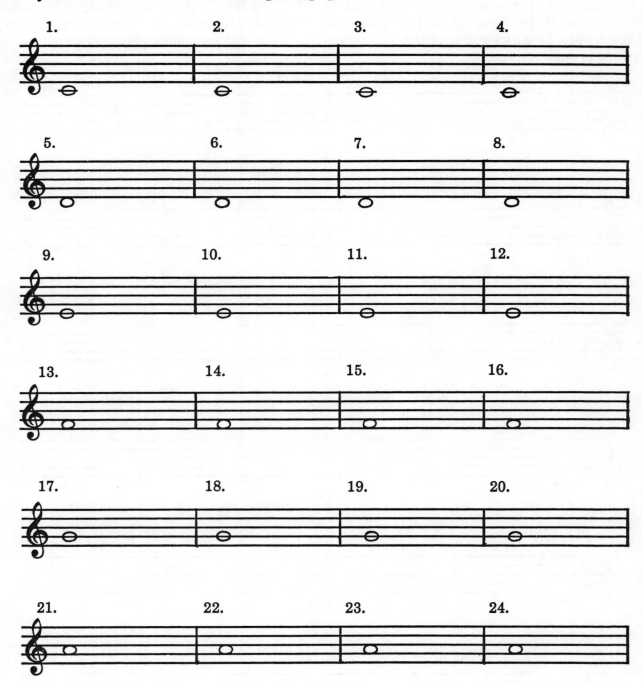

4. WHAT'S THE STEP?

(XII–4)

A HALF STEP is the distance from one key to the nearest key with no key in between.

A WHOLE STEP is the distance from one key to a neighbor key with one key in between.

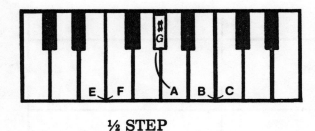

½ STEP

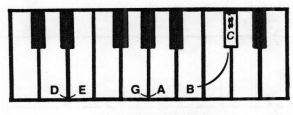

1 WHOLE STEP

For each exercise below, you will hear one note being played after the other on the keyboard. Listen carefully to each example and decide where the second note should be placed. Write the note on the staff, and the accidental, if needed.

The second note will be either a WHOLE STEP higher or a WHOLE STEP lower than the first.

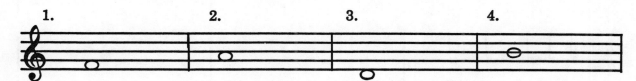

The second note will either be a HALF STEP higher or a HALF STEP lower than the first.

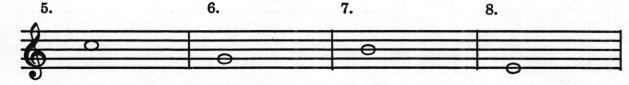

The second note will either be a HALF STEP higher or a WHOLE STEP higher than the first.

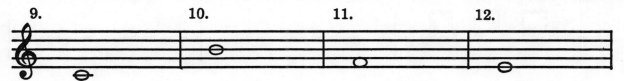

The second note will either be a HALF STEP lower or a WHOLE STEP lower than the first.

5. COMPLETE THE RHYTHM PATTERNS   (XII–5)

Listen to each rhythm pattern as it is played. Decide which notes and rests belong in measures two and three and complete the patterns.

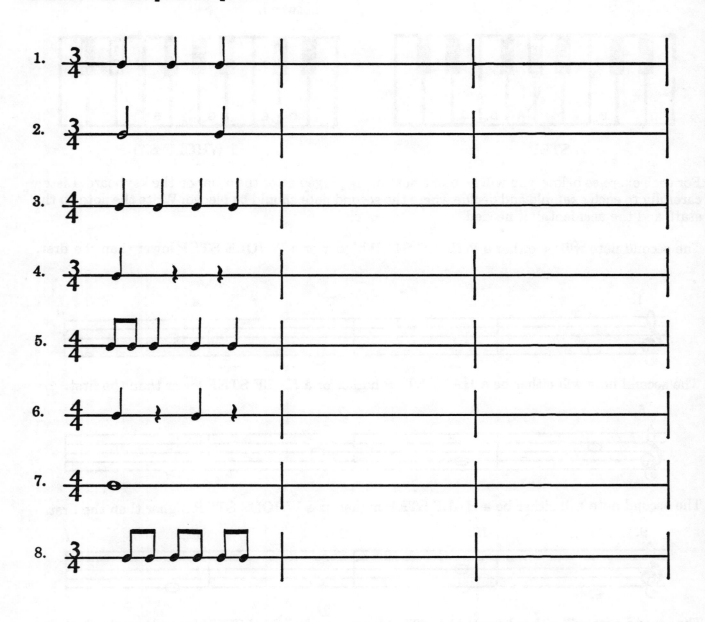

Name _____   Score _____

Date _____   Class _____

6. CHOOSE THE SONG

The beginnings of several tunes are shown below, but one measure is missing from each example. Listen carefully as you hear the melody to complete the missing measure. Then write the notes on the staff. Each tune will be played three times.

1.

2.

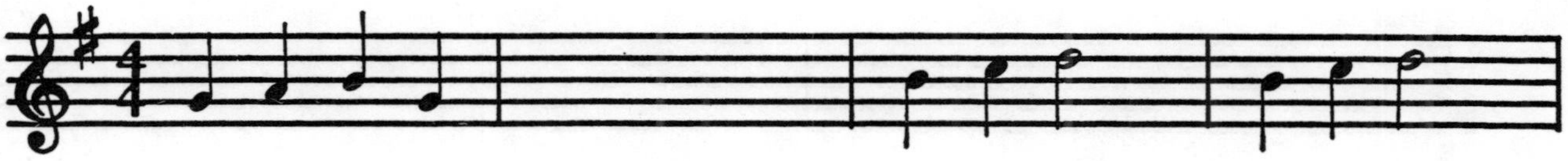

3.

4.

5.

Listen to each beginning melody again and write the name of the tune on the lines below. Choose each answer from the titles at the right.

6. _____   "Are You Sleeping?"

7. _____   "Theme from Beethoven's Ninth Symphony"

8. _____   "Merrily We Roll Along"

9. _____   "The Farmer in the Dell"

10. _____   "Yankee Doodle"

Name _____

Date _____

7. CREATE YOUR OWN MUSIC

Try your hand at composing an original tune. Be creative!

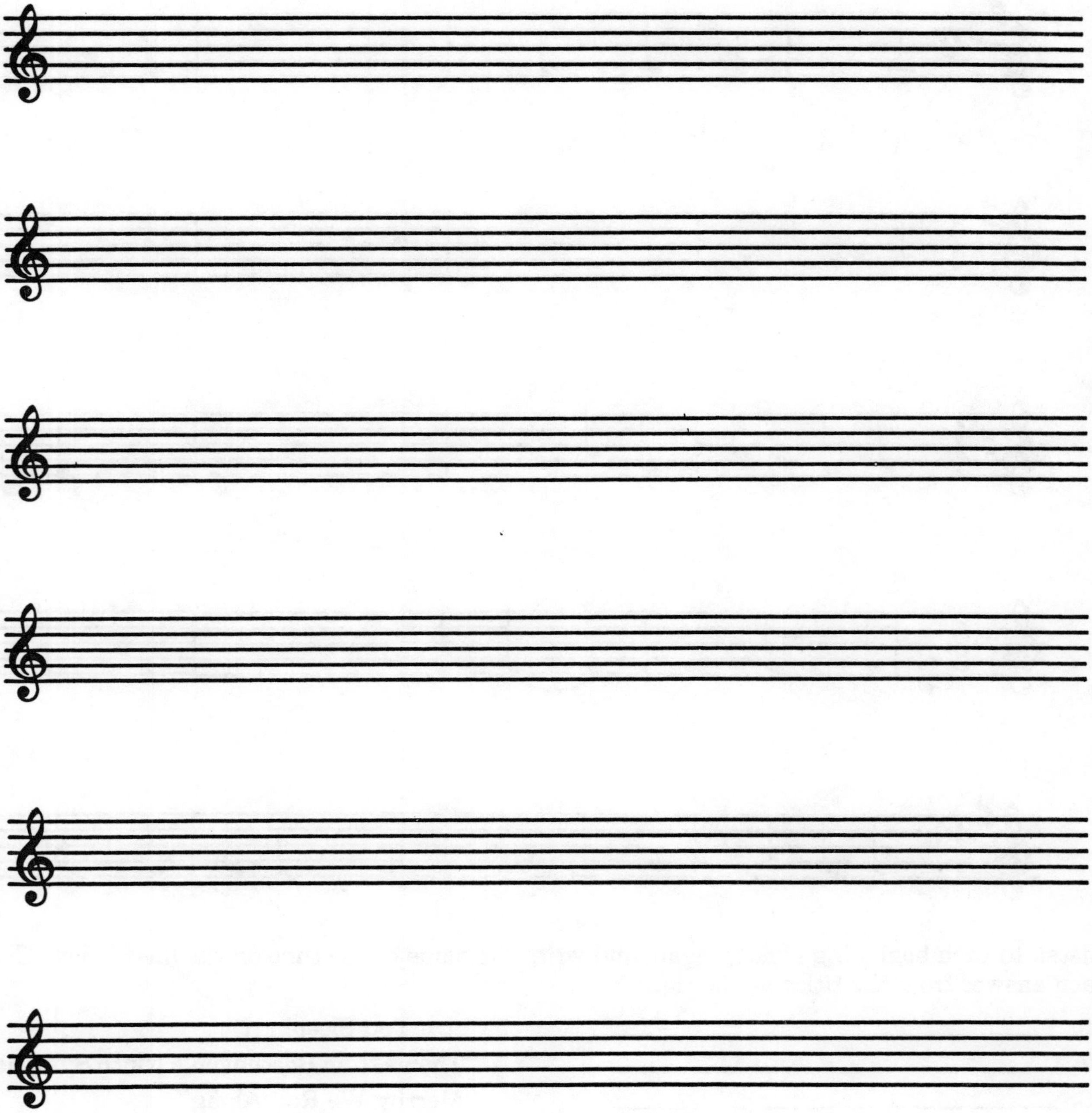

TEACHER'S GUIDE
AND ANSWER KEY

The activities in this section are designed for the teacher to create his or her own answers. These activities are intended to be used as enrichment or follow-up exercises for specific skills as indicated below.

1. *Finish the Rhythm Pattern*

   Use with Sections IV and V.

2. *Recognize the Sequence*

   Use with Sections III and VII.

3. *Hear It and Write It*

   This exercise may be used before students study note values. Sample answers:
   1. C C C   2. C D E   3. C C D   4. C D C D, etc.
   After students know the types of notes, use notes of different values in ear-training exercises.
   Use with Sections II, III, IV, V, VI, and IX.

4. *What's the Step?*

   Use with Sections VI and VII.

5. *Complete the Rhythm Patterns*

   Use with Sections IV and V.

6. *Choose the Song*

   Use with Sections IV, V, VI, VII, and IX.

7. *Create Your Own Music*

   These staff lines are to be used for melodic dictation and for students' original compositions.

Section XIII
GETTING ACQUAINTED WITH THE INSTRUMENTS

No.	Activity Title	Skill Involved
1.	CLASSIFY THE VOICES	(Grouping like singers)
2.	WHO BELONGS WHERE?	(Illustrating and naming singing groups)
3.	MATCHING CONTEST	(Matching range with voice classification)
4.	MATCH 'EM UP	(Matching missing parts with instruments)
5.	BOW, STRIKE, OR BLOW	(Classifying instruments)
6.	KNOW YOUR STRIKERS AND SHAKERS	(Matching percussion instruments with the names)
7.	KNOW YOUR PERCUSSION	(Identifying percussion instruments)
8.	BE A WOODWIND WIZARD	(Recalling facts about woodwind instruments)
9.	THE IMPACT OF BRASS	(Recalling facts about brass instruments)
10.	UNRAVEL THE STRINGS	(Recalling facts about stringed instruments)
11.	THE STRINGS PUZZLE	(Recalling facts about strings—crossword puzzle)
12.	NAME THE STRINGED INSTRUMENTS	(Naming stringed instruments and identifying members of the orchestra)
13.	PROGRAM THE PIANO	(Recalling facts about the piano)
14.	ALL IN THE FAMILY	(Classifying instruments in families)
15.	ADD 3 MORE	(Grouping similar instruments)

No.	Activity Title	Skill Involved
16.	FIND THE HIDDEN INSTRU-MENT	(Recalling facts about various instruments)
17.	DRAW THEIR INSTRUMENTS	(Illustrating various instruments)
18.	THE MUSICAL WORDFINDER RACE	(Finding names of musical instruments)
19.	THE "CASE" OF THE MISS-ING INSTRUMENT	(Drawing and naming instruments)

TEACHER'S GUIDE AND ANSWER KEY

Name _____   Score _____

Date _____   Class _____

1. CLASSIFY THE VOICES   (XIII–1)

Each singing voice has its own timbre, range, and dynamics. Draw
lines to connect the following terms with their definitions. Use the
dictionary to check your work.

1. TIMBRE   a. highness or lowness of a pitch

2. RANGE   b. loudness or softness of a tone

3. DYNAMICS   c. tone quality

Every singing voice has certain qualities. How would you describe the characteristics of your own
voice? Several traits are listed below. Underline the ones that best describe your singing voice. Add
any additional traits that may apply to your voice.

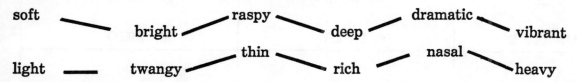

soft   raspy   dramatic
    bright   deep   vibrant
        thin   nasal
light   twangy   rich   heavy

A voice may be classified according to the style for which it is trained. Read the voice qualities
listed below and match a singer with the type of music to which he or she would perform. You may
choose your answers from the suggested singers and types of music listed.

NAMES OF SINGERS: Luciano Pavarotti, Ella Fitzgerald, Leontine Price, Johnny Cash, Dolly
                     Parton

TYPES OF MUSIC: Country Western, Opera, Rock, Blues, Jazz, Popular, Religious, Folk

VOICE QUALITIES	NAME OF SINGER	TYPE OF MUSIC
A coloratura soprano who sings rapid trills and runs.		
A lyric voice with a beautiful tone quality.		
A twangy and nasal quality of tone.		

Name _____   Score _____

Date _____   Class _____

2. *WHO BELONGS WHERE?*

1. What is a vocal solo? _____
_____
2. What is a vocal ensemble? _____
_____

Draw the correct number of faces in each section below to show how many people would be singing in the ensembles listed.

3. QUARTET	4. DUET	5. TRIO
6. SEXTET	7. QUINTET	8. OCTET

Write the correct answer under each question. You can find your answers at the right.

mixed choir
women's chorus
men's chorus
a cappella
choir

9. What is a body of church singers called?

10. What is a group of men's voices called?

11. What is a group of women's voices called?

12. What is a combination of both voices called?

13. What is it called when a person sings without an accompaniment?

3. MATCHING CONTEST

(XIII–3)

There are three types of singing voices for both the female and the male. Female voices are called SOPRANO, MEZZO-SOPRANO, and ALTO or CONTRALTO. Male voices are called TENOR, BARITONE, and BASS.

The range in pitch for both groups of voices is illustrated below on the two sets of keyboards.

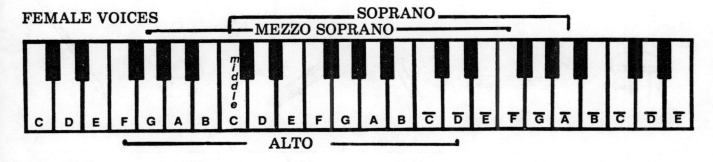

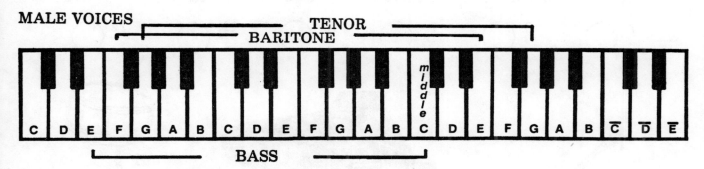

Use the keyboard charts to complete the matching activity below. Draw a line from the type of voice at the left to the correct description at the right.

1. SOPRANO   a. MALE VOICE, Low Register
2. TENOR   b. FEMALE VOICE, High Register
3. BASS   c. MALE VOICE, Medium Register
4. ALTO   d. FEMALE VOICE, Low Register
5. MEZZO SOPRANO   e. MALE VOICE, High Register
6. BARITONE   f. FEMALE VOICE, Medium Register

Name _____ Score _____

Date _____ Class _____

4. MATCH 'EM UP (XIII—4)

Each instrument on this page has an additional part. First, unscramble the names of the instrument part by writing the words on the blanks above the scrambled letters. Then match the instruments with their parts by writing the identifying letters in the circles. When you are finished, the letters will spell a musical word.

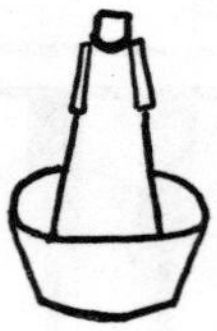

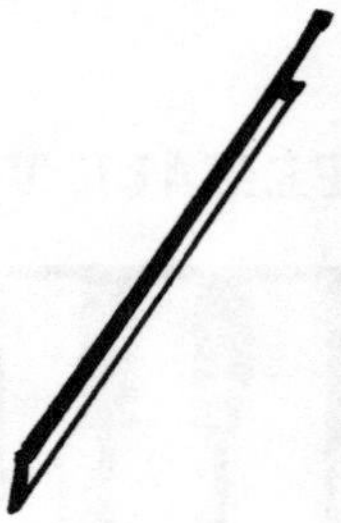

1. _____ 2. _____ 3. _____ 4. _____ 5. _____ 6. _____
   nechb   durmkictss   stelmal   dere   tume   wob

7. ◯ 8. ◯ 9. ◯ 10. ◯ 11. ◯ 12. ◯

M

Y

E

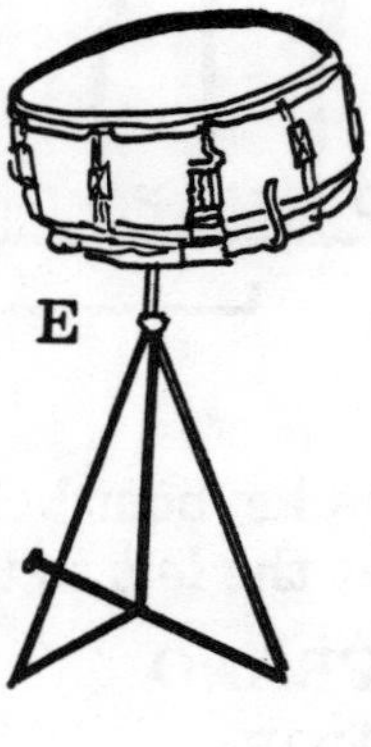

O

L

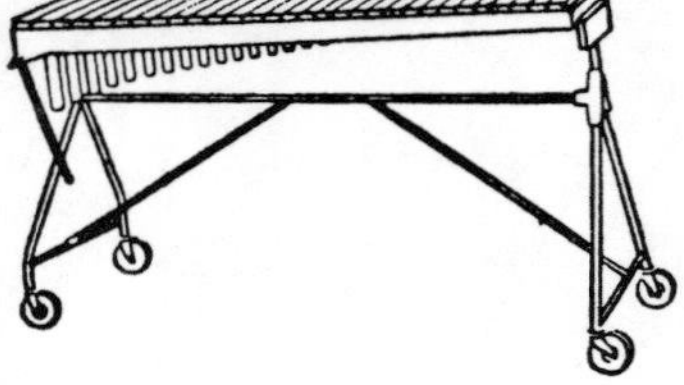

D

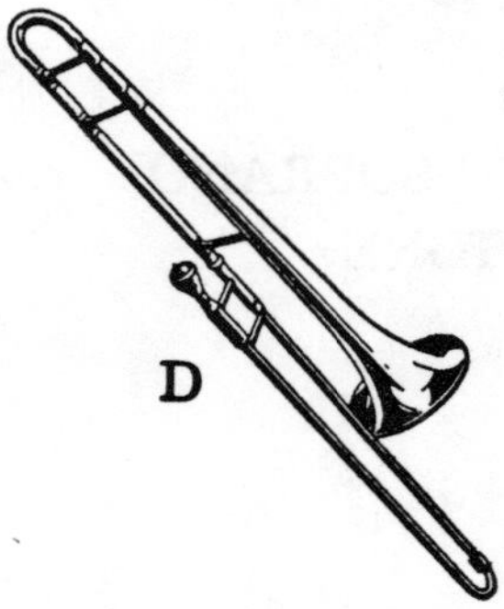

Name _____   Score _____

Date _____   Class _____

5. BOW, STRIKE, OR BLOW   (XIII–5)

Draw a line under the instruments you bow, circle the instruments you strike, and draw an "X" through the instruments you blow.

Name _____   Score _____

Date _____   Class _____

6. KNOW YOUR STRIKERS AND SHAKERS   (XIII–6)

Match each instrument to its name
by writing the identifying letter on
the blank.

_____ 1. cymbals
_____ 2. gong
_____ 3. bass drum
_____ 4. snare drum
_____ 5. timpani (kettle drums)
_____ 6. triangle
_____ 7. xylophone
_____ 8. stick castanet
_____ 9. tambourine
_____10. tone block
_____11. clave
_____12. chimes
_____13. guiro
_____14. conga drum
_____15. cow bell
_____16. maracas

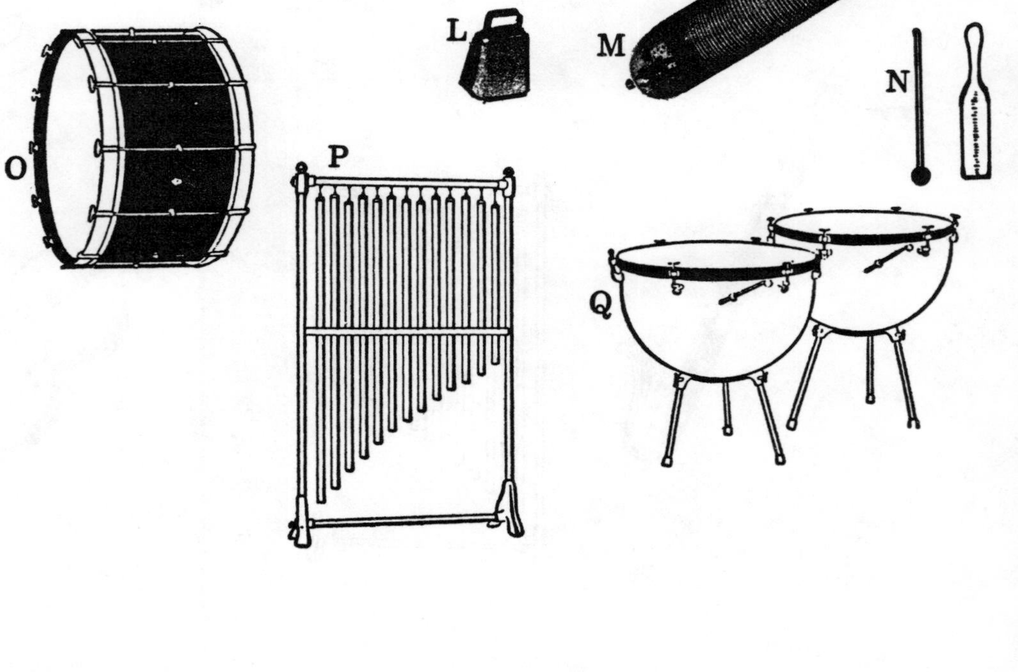

7. KNOW YOUR PERCUSSION   (XIII–7)

Identify the percussion instruments that are defined below. Fill in the blanks with the missing letters. Match the instrument with its name by writing its identifying letter in the box under the number. If you are correct, the boxed letters will spell an instrument.

1. C _ _ _ _ _ _ are hollowed brass discs. The strap to grasp them is fastened to the center of each. The player brings the edges together with a sliding motion.

2. K _ _ _ _ _ _ D _ _ _ _ are made of shiny copper covered with calfskin parchment. They are always used in pairs by a player who is skillful at tuning.

3. B _ _ _ _ D _ _ _ _ resembles a large hooplike body with a skin over each end. It's a timekeeper in an orchestra.

4. G _ _ _ comes from China. It is a large thin plate made from different metals. When it is brushed or rubbed by a soft drumstick, it makes a weird mysterious sound.

5. S _ _ _ _ _ D _ _ _ is used with two round-tipped sticks of hardwood. The drummer plays on one end of this drum.

6. T _ _ _ _ _ _ _ _ _ is the gypsy drum. It is a small wooden hoop with a skin stretched over one end with little metal jingles wired to the sides.

7. B _ _ _ _ is another name for the glockenspiel. It is an instrument made of a series of horizontal rectangular steel plates of varying lengths. The plates are arranged in the order of the piano keyboard and are struck by two wooden hammers.

8. BE A WOODWIND WIZARD   (XIII–8)

Match each instrument with its name
by writing the identifying letters on
the blank.

____ 1. oboe
____ 2. flute
____ 3. piccolo
____ 4. bassoon
____ 5. clarinet
____ 6. English horn
____ 7. bass clarinet
____ 8. contrabassoon

What facts do you know about woodwind instruments? Read the questions below and write your
answers on the blanks.

9. What is the thin strip of cane on the mouthpiece of a woodwind instrument called? _____

10. Name a woodwind instrument that uses a double reed. _____

11. When the player blows into the instrument by using the reed, what causes the column of air to

    produce a sound? _____

12. One of the instruments in this family is the oldest instrument known to man. It is played by
    blowing over an opening near one end of the tube. What instrument is it? _____

13. What is the little "sister" (or "brother") of the flute called? _____

14. What instrument was at one time referred to as the licorice stick? _____

Name _____   Score _____

Date _____   Class _____

9. THE IMPACT OF BRASS   (XIII-9)

1. Name the brass instrument that produces the highest tone. _____

2. Name the brass instrument that produces the lowest tone. _____

3. How are the lips used to produce a tone on a brass instrument? _____

4. If the lips are tightened to produce a high tone, what is done to produce a low tone on a brass instrument? _____

5. What must the air do inside the tube of a brass instrument to produce a sound? _____

6. Explain how the length of the tube of a brass instrument has a direct relationship to the pitch of the instrument. _____
_____

7. What are the knobs on the tuba, French horn and trumpet called? They are used as keys for the performer to press. _____

8. What does a trombone player use to change pitches? _____

Name these brass instruments. The answers are given in mirror language. You figure them out!

ENOBMORT
TEPMURT
ABUT
NROH HCNERF

9. _____   11. _____

10. _____   12. _____

Name _____   Score _____

Date _____   Class _____

10. UNRAVEL THE STRINGS   (XIII–10)

Use a reference book to find the answers to these questions.

1. How do you make a sound on a stringed instrument? _____
_____

2. What makes the different sounding pitches on a stringed instrument? _____
_____
_____

3. When one plays strings in order from thicker to thinner, in which direction will the pitches go?
_____

4. How do you tune a stringed instrument? _____
_____

5. What is a "fret"? _____

6. What is the "bridge" used for? _____
_____

7. How many strings does the double bass have? _____

8. How many strings does the harp have? _____

9. What stringed instruments do you find in an orchestra? _____
_____

10. Which stringed instruments are used for folk music? _____
_____

11. Name a piece of music you have listened to that features a stringed instrument. _____
_____

12. What do these famous people—Jascha Heifetz, Itzhak Perlman, and Isaac Stern—have in common? _____
Bonus: Draw your favorite stringed instrument on the back of this sheet.

11. THE STRINGS PUZZLE (XIII–11)

This puzzle tests your knowledge about the "strings." How well can you do?

ACROSS

2. The second member of the violin family is the _____.
4. Guitar music is notated one octave _____ than what it sounds.
7. The _____ is a fretted stringed instrument of the guitar family.
8. The double-_____ looks like a giant violin.
9. There are over forty _____ on the harp.
13. The modern guitar has _____ strings that are tuned: E - A - D - G - B - E.
14. A Hawaiian instrument with four strings, a long finger board, and frets is a _____.
16. A _____ piece is for a single instrument or voice.
17. You turn the pegs to _____ a stringed instrument.
20. To play a harp, you must _____ the strings.
21. One advantage of tablature is that you don't have to _____ notes.
22. The smaller the instrument, the longer the _____; the violin _____ is the longest, the bass _____ is the shortest.

DOWN

1. Antonio Stradivari built one of the most famous _____.
3. The viola is one-seventh _____ than the violin.
5. The double-bass is the _____ stringed instrument.
6. The violin comes closer to resembling the human _____ than any other instrument.
10. _____ is a method of writing music that shows hand positions instead of notes.
11. The player must be seated to play this stringed instrument.
12. The balalaika is a popular _____ instrument of the guitar family.
15. The raised lines crossing the finger board of the banjo and guitar are called _____.
18. The double-bass is also called the bass _____ or contrabasso.
19. The _____ is one of the oldest stringed instruments.
20. The strings of this keyboard instrument are struck by hammers.

Name _____   Score _____

Date _____   Class _____

12. *NAME THE STRINGED INSTRUMENTS*

Ten stringed instruments are shown on this page. Write the name of each instrument under its picture. Choose your answers from the names in the box. Then write an "X" on each instrument that is used in the symphony orchestra.

harp	cello
piano	guitar
violin	balalaika
double bass	ukulele
viola	banjo

1. _____

2. _____

3. _____

4. _____

5. _____

9. _____

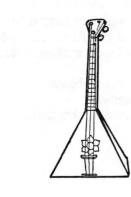

6. _____ 7. _____ 8. _____

10. _____

13. PROGRAM THE PIANO   (XIII–13)

Can you program this piano computer with the right answers? Circle the correct answer for each of the following statements. After you finish, write the identifying letter on the matching computer disc. The letter for the number 1 answer goes on the number 1 disc, the letter for the number 2 answer goes on the number 2 disc, and so on.

1. The piano may be described as a _____ instrument.
   e. brass   f. woodwind   g. keyboard
2. The strings on the piano are struck by _____.
   r. hammers   s. mallets   t. fingers
3. The _____ on the piano are stretched over the sounding-board.
   d. keys   e. strings   f. hammers
4. The small lengthy pieces of _____ covered with felt, which lie above the strings, are called dampers.
   a. wood   b. metal   c. ivory
5. Pressure on the keys sets the action mechanism to work and causes the hammers to _____ the strings.
   r. muffle   s. press   t. strike
6. The keys on the piano are generally made of acrylite, celluloid, or _____.
   o. opal   p. ivory   q. silica
7. A piano needs tuning at least _____ a year.
   h. 6 times   i. twice   j. 8 times

8. Except for the modern pipe organ, the piano is probably the only instrument today that can perform in an unaccompanied _____ recital.
   a. solo   b. melody   c. traditional
9. A standard size piano has _____ keys spanning a range of 7¼ octaves.
   l. 148   m. 124   n. 88
10. The wood, felt, and leather parts of a _____ are especially sensitive to heat and moisture. To protect the life of your piano, you must give it proper attention.
    o. piano   p. keyboard   q. sounding-board

14. ALL IN THE FAMILY   (XIII–14)

Give these instruments a home. Write the name of each instrument under the family to which it belongs. Use the diagram of the orchestra to help you identify the instruments.

NAMES OF INSTRUMENTS

glockenspiel	viola	harp	double bass	cymbals	timpani (kettle drums)
trumpet	French horn	trombone	gong	triangle	cello (violoncelli)
bass clarinet	clarinet	violin	xylophone	English horn	tone block
bassoon	maracas	piccolo	bass drum	saxophone	snare drum
contrabassoon	chimes	piano	flute	oboe	tuba

STRING	WOODWIND
BRASS	**PERCUSSION**

ORCHESTRA

Name _____   Score _____

Date _____   Class _____

15. ADD 3 MORE   (XIII–15)

Listed below are pairs of similar instruments or musical terms. To each pair add three or more similar words to make a group of five.

1.	TRUMPET	___	___	___	TUBA
2.	VIOLIN	___	___	___	DOUBLE BASS
3.	PICCOLO	___	___	___	CONTRABASSOON
4.	SNARE DRUM	___	___	___	TIMPANI
5.	PIANO	___	___	___	XYLOPHONE
6.	UKULELE	___	___	___	MANDOLIN
7.	MARACAS	___	___	___	TRIANGLE
8.	SOLO	___	___	___	QUINTET
9.	JAZZ	___	___	___	CLASSICAL
10.	SOPRANO	___	___	___	BASS
11.	KEYBOARD	___	___	___	BRASS
12.	BOW	___	___	___	PICK

16. FIND THE HIDDEN INSTRUMENT   (XIII—16)

To solve the puzzle and find the hidden instrument, color the numbered puzzle space if the statement below is true.

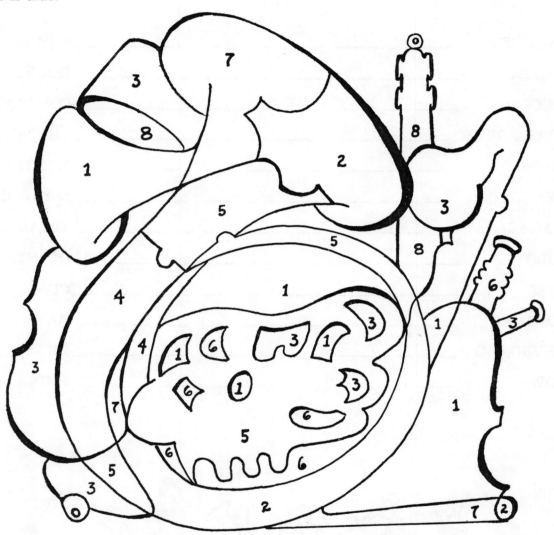

1. If a trumpet player uses a bow, color the number 1 spaces.
2. If a flute belongs to the woodwind family, color the number 2 spaces.
3. If a double bass has five strings, color the number 3 spaces.
4. If the French horn has valves, color the number 4 spaces.
5. If a conductor can be called a maestro, color the number 5 spaces.
6. If a band player uses the podium on which to lay music, color the number 6 spaces.
7. If a trombone has a slide, color the number 7 spaces.
8. If a tuba uses a reed, color the number 8 spaces.
9. Name the instrument in the puzzle.

_____

17. DRAW THEIR INSTRUMENTS   (XIII–17)

Please help these young "budding musicians" by drawing their instruments.

Philip

Karen

Mike

Mary

Reginald

Tom

Janet

Kent

Name _____   Score _____

Date _____   Class _____

18. THE MUSICAL WORDFINDER RACE

Find 35 words in this puzzle that have to do with instrumental music. The words can be found vertically, horizontally, and diagonally. When you find each word, draw a line through it.
Copy the words on a separate sheet of paper; then write them in alphabetical order on the lines at the right.

```
N B T U C L A R I N E T B L T
Z A R V N O P P G Q R S R O E
I C Q A M K E Y B O A R D I W
X C S W S T R I N G N G D F O
D Y Y X T S C D U E T G C B B
O M L O I L U H I G C E L L O
B B A O M J S A X O P H O N E
P A N R P K S R E E D S O A Z
O L N D A H I P W T P X O R Y
S S T D N W O O D W I N D L N
I C R A I U N N F G A M L S O
T O O T C H I M E S N V P N K
R U M R O R G A N H O I I A J
U F B C E V B A S S O O N R X
M L O A B A S S V I O L M E P
P U N V I O L I N P O A N D L
E T E U T R O R C H E S T R A
T E V T A M B O U R I N E U Y
M A R C H S B A S S D R U M Q
```

1. _____
2. _____
3. _____
4. _____
5. _____
6. _____
7. _____
8. _____
9. _____
10. _____
11. _____
12. _____
13. _____
14. _____
15. _____
16. _____
17. _____
18. _____
19. _____
20. _____
21. _____
22. _____
23. _____
24. _____
25. _____
26. _____
27. _____
28. _____
29. _____
30. _____
31. _____
32. _____
33. _____
34. _____
35. _____

19. THE "CASE" OF THE MISSING INSTRUMENT   (XIII–19)

Below are several instrument cases. Read each description carefully. Then write the name of the instrument on the line and draw a picture of it in its case.

1. _____

The instrument that fits in this case has four strings and a bow. It is the lowest sounding of the string family.

2. _____

This instrument is brass and has a large bell-like appearance. It is derived from the 17th century hunting horn.

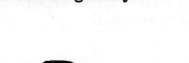

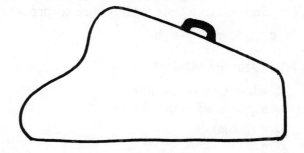

3. _____

This instrument is the highest-pitched instrument in the band or orchestra.

4. _____

This is the most ancient type of instrument still in use. The player plucks the strings of this very large instrument.

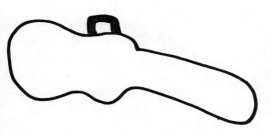

5. _____

This stringed instrument has six strings. Chords can be played on it.

6. _____

This percussion instrument is sometimes referred to as a side drum. It is played with two wooden drumsticks.

TEACHER'S GUIDE AND ANSWER KEY

1. Classify the Voices

Discuss physical requirements for good singing: (a) Stress good posture while sitting with feet on the floor and weight of the body somewhat forward, not leaning back on the chair. One should sit up straight. While standing, place the weight of the body toward the toes, rather than on the heels. (b) Encourage abdominal breathing for a controlled, continuous flow of breath. (c) Sing with an "open throat," which is an open, relaxed throat when ready to yawn. (d) Enunciate words, being sure to pronounce final consonants clearly.

1. c   2. a.   3. b.

2. Who Belongs Where?

1. when one sings alone
2. a group of singers
3. 4 (faces)
4. 2
5. 3
6. 6
7. 5
8. 8
9. choir
10. men's chorus
11. women's chorus
12. mixed choir
13. a cappella

3. Matching Contest

1. b
2. e
3. a
4. d
5. f
6. c

4. Match 'Em Up

1. bench   2. drumsticks   3. mallets   4. reed   5. mute   6. bow
7. M (piano)   8. E (snare drum)   9. L (xylophone)   10. O (clarinet)   11. D (trombone)
12. Y (violin)

5. Bow, Strike, or Blow

1. line – viola
2. "X" – flute
3. circle – cow bell
4. circle – wood blocks
5. "X" – melodica
6. circle – tambourine
7. "X" – trumpet
8. "X" – recorder
9. circle – bass drum
10. circle –cymbals
11. "X" –bass clarinet
12. circle – chimes
13. line – double bass
14. circle – triangle

6. Know Your Strikers and Shakers

1. B
2. C
3. O
4. H
5. Q
6. G
7. E
8. I
9. F
10. K
11. J
12. P
13. M
14. A
15. L
16. D

7. Know Your Percussion

The word percussion comes from a Latin word meaning to "hit or strike." The instruments in this section of the orchestra are played by striking, shaking, banging, and tapping.

Discuss the two basic types of percussion instruments: (1) those that have pitch, including the tympani or kettle drums, chimes, xylophone, glockenspiel, celesta, marimba, bells, and piano; (2) the striking instruments used to create special effects or accent rhythm. Instruments in this category are the drums, gongs, wood blocks, castanets, tambourines, cymbals, triangles, and maracas. Explain how a piano is a percussion instrument that can also belong to the string family.

Make simple percussion instruments for a rhythm band. Look for objects that would make good percussion sounds. Add dry rice to small milk cartons for shakers; cover margarine tubs or oatmeal boxes with stretched inner tubing for drums.

1. C cymbals
2. Y kettle drums
3. M bass drum
4. B gong
5. A snare drum
6. L tambourine
7. S bells

8. Be a Woodwind Wizard

The woodwind instruments are very different among themselves. To produce a tone on the flute or piccolo, the player blows across a hole in the side of the tube near the top. Air vibrates in the tube causing the sound. The piccolo is the tiniest instrument of the orchestra and makes the highest sound. Piccolos and flutes are usually made of metal.

The clarinet uses a piece of cane reed fastened to the mouthpiece. When the player blows, the single reed vibrates and causes the air to vibrate and make a sound. The clarinet, generally made of ebonite, has a larger range than most instruments.

The oboe, English horn, and bassoon are called double reed instruments. Their sounds are made by blowing air between two very thin reeds which are attached together. The highest sounding and smallest of the double reeds is the oboe. The contrabassoon is the lowest sounding instrument in the orchestra. The player covers and uncovers the holes with metal keys on the instrument to produce a sound. When the air vibrates between the mouthpiece and the nearest hole in the tube, the sound is either high or low depending on how far the air has to travel.

1. D	6. H	10. oboe, English horn, bassoon, and contrabassoon
2. B	7. G	11. the air vibrates
3. A	8. E	12. flute
4. F	9. reed	13. piccolo
5. C		14. clarinet

9. The Impact of Brass

Brass instruments are just as important to the symphony orchestra as they are to the band. The trumpet is the smallest instrument of the brass family and the highest sounding. Its sound is brilliant and is often heard playing fanfares. The French horn is more mellow in tone. It is constructed from 16 feet of brass tubing twisted into coils that flare out into a wide bell. The trombone is the most powerful of all the instruments of the orchestra. One can easily identify the low tone of the trombone because of the slide. The trombone is the only instrument that changes size while it is being played. The performer pushes the sliding tube in to produce high tones and pushes it out to produce low tones. The tuba is an easy instrument to identify because of its very low pitch.

To produce a tone on a brass instrument, the player must tighten his or her lips while putting them against the cup-shaped mouthpiece, and blow air through his or her lips into the mouthpiece. This vibration of the lips, together with the blowing of the right amount of air into the instrument, produces a tone.

1. trumpet   2. tuba   3. (see above)   4. loosen   5. vibrate   6. (see above)
7. valves   8. slide   9. trumpet   10. French horn   11. trombone   12. tuba.

10. Unravel the Strings

String instruments resemble each other. The violin is the highest sounding and is the smallest in size, about two feet long. The viola is just slightly larger in size and sounds a little lower. The violin and viola are both held with the left hand and tucked under the chin when played. To play a cello, the performer must sit on a chair and rest the cello on the floor. The double bass or contrabasso is six feet tall and the lowest sounding of the string family. The violin, viola, cello, and double bass all belong to the bowed string class of instruments. However, a wide variety of tone qualities can be produced using other methods than bowing. One method is called "pizzicato" which means plucking the strings. The harp is considered the most ancient type of instrument still in use and produces a tone by plucking the strings.

1. A tone is produced by means of the vibrations of a stretched string. On a bowed string instrument, the player draws a bow across the strings. To get different notes, she presses the string against the fingerboard with her finger, changing the length of the string. On a plucked string instrument, the player plucks the strings with her fingers or with a pick.

2. The performer presses the string against the fingerboard with his finger, changing the length of the string. The shorter the string, the more rapid the vibrations. The quicker the vibrations, the higher the sound.

3. higher

4. violin—G̲ D A̲ E, Viola—C̲ G̲ D A, Cello—C̲ G̲ D̲ A̲, Bass—E̲ A̲ D G, Guitar—E̲ A̲ D G B E̲. (1 line above the letter = high C̄ or higher; 1 line below the letter = a note

lower than middle C; 2 lines below the letter = a note an octave lower than middle C)
Several methods may be used to tune a guitar. A beginning guitarist will find tuning to
the keys of a piano or to a pitchpipe easiest.

5. Frets are the raised lines across the fingerboard of stringed instruments, such as a lute,
   guitar, viol, balalaika, and banjo, which mark the position for the stopping of the strings.

6. The strings are stretched across this wooden support.

7. four

8. over forty

9. violin, viola, cello, contrabasso, harp, and piano

10. lute, guitar, ukulele, banjo, autoharp, and balalaika

11. Answers will vary.

12. They are all violinists.

11. *The Strings Puzzle*

12. Name the Stringed Instruments

1. violin X
2. viola X
3. cello X
4. double bass X
5. harp X
6. guitar
7. banjo
8. balalaika
9. piano X
10. ukulele

13. Program the Piano

The piano is a familiar instrument with most children. Because you strike the keys on the piano to produce a tone, it is classified as a percussion instrument. However, the piano also has strings to make its own rhythm, harmony, and melody.

1. g   2. r   3. e   4. a   5. t   6. p   7. i   8. a   9. n   10. o

14. All in the Family

A symphony orchestra usually has about 100 instruments. More than half of them are strings. There are four sections or families in the orchestra: the strings, woodwind, brass, and percussion.

STRING: viola, harp, violin, double bass, cello

WOODWIND: bass clarinet, clarinet, flute, English horn, saxophone, piccolo, bassoon, contra-bassoon, oboe

BRASS: trumpet, French horn, trombone, tuba

PERCUSSION: glockenspiel, maracas, chimes, piano, gong, xylophone, cymbals, triangle, timpani, tone block, snare drum

15. Add 3 More

(Suggested answers)
1. flügelhorn, cornet, French horn
2. viola, cello, guitar
3. flute, clarinet, oboe
4. bongo, bass drum, kettle drums
5. marimba, harpsichord, glockenspiel
6. banjo, guitar, balalaika
7. castanets, wood blocks, claves
8. duet, trio, quartet
9. folk, rock, blues
10. alto, tenor, baritone
11. percussion, strings, woodwind
12. finger-board, peg, bridge

16. Find the Hidden Instrument

1. False   2. True   3. False   4. True   5. True   6. False
7. True   8. False   9. French horn

17. Draw Their Instruments

Suggested instruments: Philip – trombone, Karen – harp, Mike – violin, Mary – flute, Reginald – piano, Tom – banjo, Janet – timpani, Kent – double bass. (Reginald, Tom, Janet, and Kent could all be playing instruments other than the ones listed.)

18. The Musical Wordfinder Race

1. band	8. chimes	15. keyboard	22. play	29. tambourine
2. bass drum	9. clarinet	16. march	23. reed	30. timpani
3. bassoon	10. cymbals	17. oboe	24. saxophone	31. trio
4. bass viol	11. duet	18. orchestra	25. score	32. trombone
5. bow	12. flute	19. organ	26. snare drum	33. trumpet
6. brass	13. harp	20. percussion	27. solo	34. tuba
7. cello	14. horn	21. piano	28. string	35. viola
				36. violin
				37. woodwind
				38. xylophone

19. The "Case" of the Missing Instrument

1. double bass   2. French horn   3. piccolo   4. harp   5. guitar
6. snare drum

Section XIV
JUST FOR FUN

TEACHER'S GUIDE AND ANSWER KEY

1. ANSWER BY CODE   (XIV-1)

Which instrument shall I learn to play? You may need to consider these criteria. Some instruments require certain characteristics, abilities, and talents. Match the instrument with the requirement by writing the name of the instrument on the line next to the requirement. Check your answers with the number code at the bottom of this page.

8 13 26 9 22 23 9 6 14
_____

5 18 12 15 18 13
_____

19 26 9 11
_____

21 15 6 7 22
_____

11 18 26 13 12
_____

7 9 12 14 25 12 13 22
_____

12 9 20 26 13
_____

12 25 12 22
_____

7 9 6 14 11 22 7
_____

20 6 18 7 26 9
_____

1. This percussion instrument requires a good sense of rhythm along with hand coordination.
2. You need a sharp ear to match the exact pitch on the strings and to hear the tone quality while bowing. You also need to be agile from the fingers on up to the shoulders.
3. You need a keen ear to tune the instrument's 43 strings.
4. You must have the ability to direct a small stream of air across a hole on the mouthpiece of this instrument.
5. The ability to coordinate fingers, hands and arms with the distance between the keyboard and the music is a must.
6. To play this instrument, you must have an alert ear to help move the slide to the exact position along with long arms to reach out the full length for the slide.
7. Hand-and-foot coordination is needed when playing the keyboards and pedals on this instrument.
8. Lip control and nimble fingers are called for when learning to play this double-reed instrument.
9. This brass instrument is held straight out in front of the player.
10. You must have a quick, alert ear to change chords while playing a song with this instrument.

A	B	C	D	E	F	G	H	I	J	K	L	M
26	25	24	23	22	21	20	19	18	17	16	15	14
N	O	P	Q	R	S	T	U	V	W	X	Y	Z
13	12	11	10	9	8	7	6	5	4	3	2	1

Name _____   Score _____

Date _____   Class _____

2. *THINGS I FORGOT TO REMEMBER*   *(XIV-2)*

Perhaps you have forgotten the answers to some of the following questions. If so, where would you go or where would you look in your community to find the answers? Answer the questions briefly and be specific.

1. Where to buy an autoharp pick? _____

2. Where to find new strings for my guitar? _____

3. Where to locate a book on the life of Mozart? _____

4. Where to purchase an album with the latest number one hit? _____

5. Where to see an authentic harpsichord? _____

6. Where to purchase tickets for the symphony concert? _____

7. Where to see an opera? _____

8. Who to call about tuning my piano? _____

9. Where to get more information about the junior high school music program?

   _____

10. Which radio station to listen to for the best bluegrass music?

    _____

11. Who to ask about getting someone to give me piano lessons?

    _____

12. Where to order a flute solo by J.S. Bach with piano accompaniment?

    _____

13. Where to find out which rock song is number one this week?

    _____

14. Where to find out how many private music studios there are in my town?

    _____

15. Where to find out the names of the recording companies in the United States?

    _____

Name _____   Score _____

Date _____   Class _____

3. A HALLOWEEN CROSSWORD   (XIV-3)

ACROSS

2. f forte) = _____.
6. 𝄞 = _____ Clef.
7. 𝅝 = _____ Note.
8. Allegro = _____.
10. "Stars and Stripes Forever" is a _____.
12. The cello belongs to the _____ family.
14. 𝄢 , _____ C.
17. p (piano) = _____.
18. A writer of music.
22. ⁴⁄⁴ = _____ Time.
23. High female voice.
24. The staff spaces spell _____.
26. Forerunner of jazz.
28. 𝄢 _____ C.
32. ▥▥▥
33. ³⁄₄ = Triple _____.
35. A group playing instruments.
36. All singing the same tune.

DOWN

1. ♩ = _____ Note.
3. There is a Half _____ between E and F.
4. The clarinet belongs to the _____ family.
5. The distance between two bar lines.
9. The tuba is a member of the _____ family.
11. Fermata.
13. ▬ ▬ ⁷ ⁷
15. Look out for flying _____ on Halloween.
16. Provides the "background" to a melody.
19. ː‖

20. Drums are members of the _____ family.
21. Low female voice.
22. There are ghosts in _____ lit places.
25. High male voice.
27. ⌒
29. Keynote.
30. The difference in pitch between two notes.
31. Means "tail" in music.
34. Fine = The _____.

Name _____   Score _____

Date _____   Class _____

4. HOLIDAY SCRAMBLE

These song titles are all for special days of the year. The
words of the songs are in order, but they are scrambled. Can
you unscramble them?

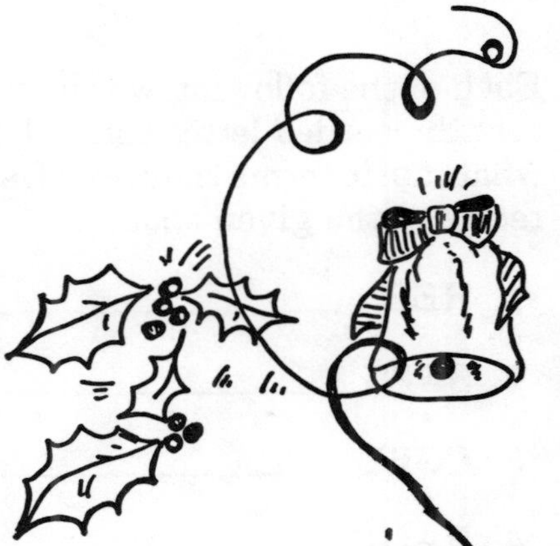

1. KNAHUHAK _____

2. VIRSEL LEBLS _____

3. GLENJI SLELB _____

4. LAUD GANL SYEN _____

5. ANSTA SLACU SI GMINOC OT WONT _____

6. STROFY HET WONSNAM _____

7. I WAS MMMYO SINGKSI ANSTA LAUSC _____

8. POLRUHD HET DER-NOESD NEDEREIR _____

9. PU NO HET SOUEHOPT _____

10. HILEW SHIRI SEEY RAE LISIGMN _____

11. REVO HET VIRER NAD TOHURHG HET DOWOS _____

12. OYUER A GNARD LOD GLAF _____

13. REHE OMCES REPET TOCOTNLAIT _____

14. NAYEKE ODOELD _____

Name _____   Score _____

Date _____   Class _____

5. THE CASE OF THE MISSING LETTERS   (XIV-5)

Each of the following words is a music term with a missing letter. Leave the letters in order and insert the needed letter somewhere in the middle, at the beginning, or at the end. Can you figure out what music terms they are? Use the "Helpful Hints" for finding your answers. Write the words correctly in the given spaces.

1. RED _____

2. SEPS _____

3. CORE _____

4. RAGE _____

5. SALE _____

6. PEAL _____

7. ITCH _____

8. SPINE _____

9. RIO _____

10. TUB _____

11. SUIT _____

12. OLD _____

13. RUM _____

14. SIDE _____

HELPFUL HINTS

1. A thin piece of wood used in the mouthpiece of a clarinet.
2. In a scalewise movement in music, the tones go up or down by these.
3. Musical notation showing all the parts for performers is written on this.
4. This term denotes the extent of how high or low a voice can sing or an instrument can play.
5. A series of tones arranged in steps.
6. A mechanism of the piano, organ or harp, worked by the foot.
7. The degree of highness or lowness of sound.
8. The name given to a modern small upright piano.
9. Three people performing as a musical group.
10. The lowest-pitched brass wind instrument.
11. A composition with a number of pieces.
12. Another name for "fermata."
13. A percussion instrument.
14. Part of a trombone.

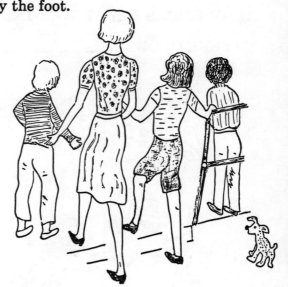

6. HIDDEN ANAGRAMS   (XIV-6)

Add a letter at the beginning or at the end of each word to make a music term. Then write the definition of each term on the space provided.

1. NTHEM _____
   _____

2. TON _____
   _____

3. RILL _____
   _____

4. METE _____
   _____

5. UTE _____

6. NOT _____

7. DUE _____

8. FORT _____

9. BLUE _____

10. COD _____

11. FIN _____

12. COMB _____

13. PACE _____

14. EAT _____

15. CELL _____

16. LENT _____

17. AND _____

18. HARP _____

Name _____   Score _____

Date _____   Class _____

7. CAN YOU CLIMB THIS TREE?

(XIV-7)

You can make it to the top of this tree if you can correctly match each symbol in the song to a term on the tree trunk. Write the number of the symbol on the matching tree step.

Letter Names

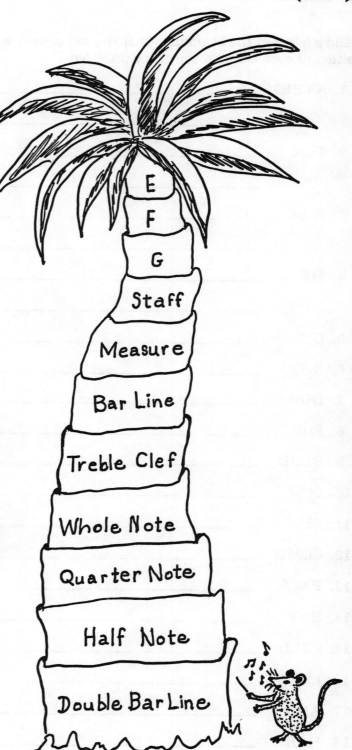

8. A CROSSWORD PUZZLE FOR THE WISE   (XIV-8)

ACROSS

4. The trumpet belongs to the _____ family.
6. A popular song is called a _____.
7. A work (musical).
9. Another name for the "G" clef.
10. The piano, bells, and guitar are all musical _____.
12. The following is a _____ note: ♩
15. Parade music: "Washington Post _____."
18. The spaces on a staff spell "_____."
19. A set of tuned tube-shaped bells.
20. The bass clef is for _____ notes.

DOWN

1. Scott _____, the "Father of Ragtime."
2. A woodwind instrument.
3. ≡ is called a _____.
5. The violin is a _____ instrument.
6. The following is a _____ note: ♩
8. Music is divided into _____.
11. The "March King."
13. A thin piece of wood used in some woodwinds.
14. A style of popular music.
16. Name the sign: ☊
17. The stick used to play a violin.

Name _____

Date _____

9. HOCUS-POCUS HOMONYMS

You are the magician's helper. Your job is to put the right homonyms into the hat. After you have filled in the correct answer, write the matching letter on the hat. You've completed your job when the letters spell the magic words.

1. A group of three or more tones played together is called a _____.
   (m) chord   (n) cord

2. A double _____ is used on the oboe.
   (t) read   (u) reed

3. Beethoven wrote in a different musical _____ from Mozart.
   (l) stile   (m) style

4. A _____ is a musical composition in which all the parts have the same melody throughout and imitate each other very strictly.
   (b) canon   (c) cannon

5. The _____ is a type of sacred music of the German Protestant Church, developed during the Baroque period.
   (n) corral   (o) chorale

6. A _____ can be an organized group of singers or instrumentalists.
   (j) choir   (k) quire

7. The lowest and largest member of the strings is the double _____.
   (t) base   (u) bass

8. A composition consisting of a number of instrumental pieces is a _____.
   (l) sweet   (m) suite

9. A count in music is referred to as the _____.
   (a) beet   (b) beat

10. A type of dance using pantomime and movement to tell a story is a _____.
    (n) belly   (o) ballet

10. CROSSWORD PUZZLE   *(XIV-10)*

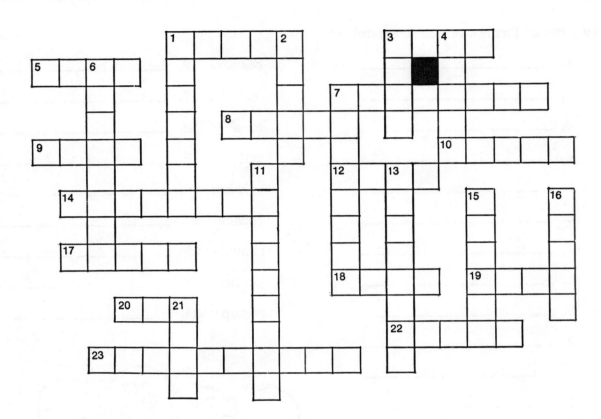

ACROSS

1. A music term meaning soft.
3. Pianissimo means very ____.
5. A silent beat in music.
7. Stephen Foster composed "My Old ____ Home."
8. CDEFGABC is called a ____.
9. A member of the percussion family.
10. Two half notes ____ one whole note.
12. The ____ clef means lower tones.
14. The distance between two notes.
17. Another term for time signature.
18. Music for two performers.
19. A sound with definite pitch.
20. A ____ after a note makes it half again as long.
22. Three or more tones sounded together.
23. Composer of "Carnival of Animals."

DOWN

1. Recordings on the "top ten" are the most ____ ones.
2. A keyboard instrument.
3. ____ a song.
4. A high-pitched woodwind instrument.
6. A melody repeated at a different pitch.
7. What the piano and melodica have in common.
11. A symphony is this type of music.
13. Same as Number 6.
15. A popular six-stringed instrument.
16. To become a good reader of music, you must learn your ____.
21. A good singer sings in ____.

11. UNSCRAMBLE THE MUSIC TERMS   (XIV-11)

How many music terms can you unscramble?

fsaft   1. _____

lefc   2. _____

retem   3. _____

nosg   4. _____

cimus   5. _____

psarh   6. _____

toen   7. _____

lelb   8. _____

toal   9. _____

lodh   10. _____

oslo   11. _____

urls   12. _____

toinc   13. _____

jorma   14. _____

etdu   15. _____

seamreu 16. _____

irutadon 17. _____

ascel   18. _____

talf   19. _____

ythrhm   20. _____

ruchos   21. _____

rimon   22. _____

poetm   23. _____

restop   24. _____

12. SYMBOL SPRINKLE   (XIV-12)

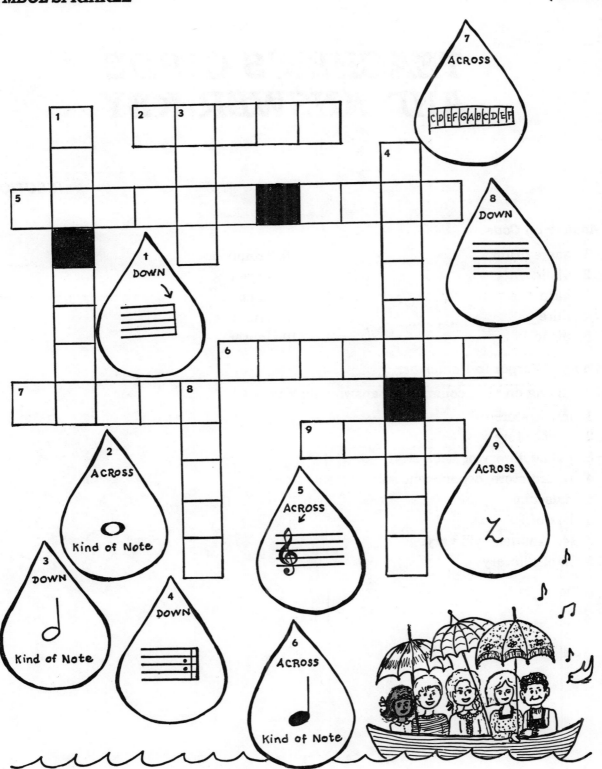

TEACHER'S GUIDE AND ANSWER KEY

1. Answer by Code

1. snare drum
2. violin
3. harp
4. flute
5. piano
6. trombone
7. organ
8. oboe
9. trumpet
10. guitar

2. Things I Forgot to Remember

(Depending on your community, answers may vary.)

1. music store
2. music store
3. public library or book store
4. record store, department store, music store
5. museum
6. box office
7–14. Answers will vary.
15. public library

3. A Halloween Crossword

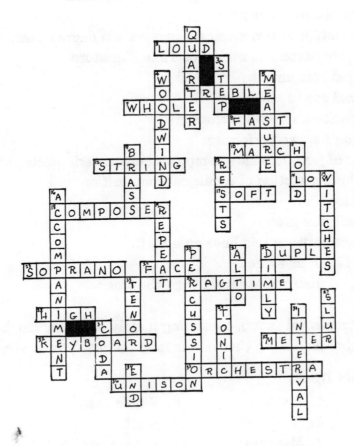

4. Holiday Scramble

1. "Hanukkah"
2. "Silver Bells"
3. "Jingle Bells"
4. "Auld Lang Syne"
5. "Santa Claus Is Coming to Town"
6. "Frosty the Snowman"
7. "I Saw Mommy Kissing Santa Claus"
8. "Rudolph the Red-Nosed Reindeer"
9. "Up on the Housetop"
10. "While Irish Eyes Are Smiling"
11. "Over the River and Through the Woods"
12. "You're a Grand Old Flag"
13. "Here Comes Peter Cottontail"
14. "Yankee Doodle"

5. The Case of the Missing Letters

1. reed
2. steps
3. score
4. range
5. scale
6. pedal
7. pitch
8. spinet
9. trio
10. tuba
11. suite
12. hold
13. drum
14. slide

6. Hidden Anagrams

1. anthem – a sacred song usually sung by a church choir
2. tone – sound of a definite pitch
3. trill – the alternation of two musical tones a scale degree apart
4. meter – rhythmic pattern in music, or Time Signature
5. lute – a stringed instrument
6. note – a musical sound
7. duet – a composition for two performers
8. forte – direction for two performers
9. blues – a style of jazz, in a slow tempo and characteristically sad
10. coda – a concluding section of a musical composition; tail
11. fine – end or close
12. combo – a small jazz group
13. space – distance between two lines on a staff
14. beat – pulse of each measure
15. cello – a stringed instrument larger than the violin
16. lento – slow
17. band – an instrumental group, consisting mainly of woodwind, brass, and percussion
18. sharp – a symbol indicating that a tone is to be raised by ½ step

7. Can You Climb This Tree?

1. Treble Clef
2. Quarter note
3. Half note
4. G
5. F
6. E
7. Measure
8. Bar line
9. Whole note
10. Staff
11. Double bar line

* Discover the melody moves by steps. Sing the melody by numbers or syllables.

8. A Crossword Puzzle for the Wise

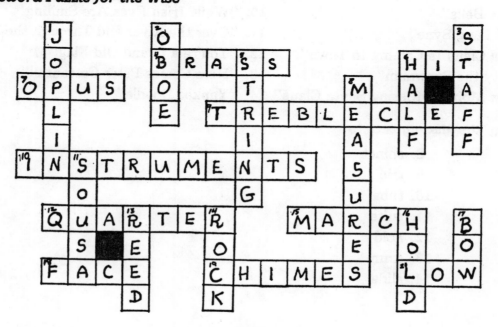

290

9. Hocus-Pocus Homonyms

1. m   2. u   3. m   4. b   5. o   6. j   7. u   8. m   9. b   10. o

10. Crossword Craze

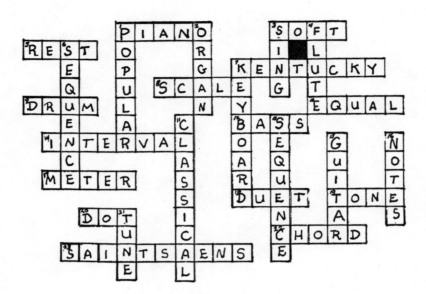

11. Unscramble the Music Terms

1. staff
2. clef
3. meter
4. song
5. music
6. sharp
7. note
8. bell
9. alto
10. hold
11. solo
12. slur
13. tonic
14. major
15. duet
16. measure
17. duration
18. scale
19. flat
20. rhythm
21. chorus
22. minor
23. tempo
24. presto

12. Symbol Sprinkle

Numbers 1, 4, and 5 each contain two words separated by a darkened square.

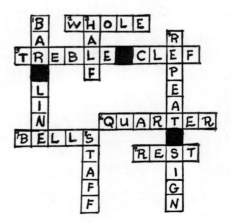